Michael D. Barnes, A.I.A.

Arise & Build

MASTERING THE REALITIES OF CHURCH BUILDING

Published by:

Integrity Enterprise, LLC
Virginia Beach, VA 23452

PRINTED IN THE UNITED STATES OF AMERICA

ISBN 0-9755687-0-1

For more information regarding the book, distribution, professional
consultation or seminars, contact the author at 1-800-530-1505.
Or reach us on the Internet at www.barnesdesigngroup.com.

Soli Deo Gloria

Endorsements

"Michael Barnes is more than an architect, he is a man committed to Jesus Christ. His vision for local church growth and evangelism is exciting. As he designs, his thoughts are on how we can reach and minister to those who have never heard or responded to the Gospel."
— **Pastor T. A. Powell**

"What we have discovered in working with Michael Barnes is a healthy balance between service of the highest quality and rare spiritual insight into the unique needs of churches."
— **Dr. Donald W. Mills, PhD.**
Pastor, Grace Bible Church

"In all my years of ministry, I have never seen a better job of 'making the vision plain'. They (renderings and design) capture not only a picture of a church, but the heart of our church toward our calling."
— **Pastor A. Ray Rouson**
1st Pentecostal United Holy

"Michael Barnes has provided first-class service in designing buildings for Calvary Revival Church over the last 10 years...As the years have passed, my confidence in him has grown, as he has consistently surpassed our expectations with his cutting-edge designs."
— **Pastor B. Courtney McBath**
Calvary Revival Church

"Working with you and your staff...has been a time of spiritual growth, partnership, church design, and leadership development, as well as master planning for the future of Faith Alive Ministries."
— **Pastor Bob Groves**
Faith Alive Ministries

Acknowledgements

This book would not be complete without acknowledging the many people who have contributed to its success. This would include my partners, associates and all of the team players at Barnes Design Group.

A heartfelt thank you to Candice Barnes, my wife, who has been a loyal supporter for over 30 years. Her faithful and loyal belief in me and in God's plan for our life has been instrumental in all the accomplishments that we have experienced.

I would also like to acknowledge and thank all of the pastors who have contributed to this book by allowing Barnes Design Group to serve them over the last 25 years. We owe a deep debt of gratitude to all of our firm's more than 300 church clients.

A special thanks goes to Andrea Page who has worked diligently to coordinate the day-to-day tasks involved in the printing and publishing of a manual such as this. She has spent many hours toiling over the manuscript and checking the chapters page by page and I am deeply indebted to her for this.

This effort would have been difficult without the assistance of Tom Powell, Brian Forrester and the complete team of The Addison Group. Their editing, attention to detail and preparation for printing were invaluable. Through their unique vision and foresight, they reminded me again and again regarding the valuable resource this book will be in the hands of pastors struggling to master the challenges of church building. It was their prayer as well as ours that the book be utilized to further the Kingdom of God.

My ultimate thanks go to God who has guided us and directed us along the way. He has blessed our efforts, added to our wisdom when we asked, expanded our territory and always been there. Without His faithful love and guidance, this work would have never been possible.

Michael D. Barnes, A.I.A.

CONTENTS

FOREGROUND
Introduction to Barnes Design Group

SPECIALISTS IN CHURCH DESIGN

Twenty-five years ago, I was just graduating from Virginia Tech's graduate department with my Master's Degree in Architecture. I had spent the last 7 years studying in two major universities and was excited to begin my career as a professional architect.

My wife, Candice, and I were certain that God had led us to Virginia Tech from the University of Kansas where I had previously received my Bachelor Degree in Architecture. That much was sure. We had married right out of high school, and we were now excited to begin our new life together outside of the university setting.

We prayed that God would lead us from the school in the Blue Ridge to that special place He had prepared for the two of us. We had matured spiritually over the last five years of marriage and were ready to serve God as he directed.

We were guided by God to relocate to Virginia Beach where the first of our four children was born directly upon our arrival. I was employed for one year by a local architectural company and then joined and became a partner of a Virginia Beach firm.

THE FIRST CHURCH PROJECT

As a young architect, I continued to serve the community by providing numerous architectural services to a variety of clients including federal government projects, school projects, Navy projects, restaurant projects, industrial projects, shopping centers and apartments and hotels.

Then one day, the church my wife and I were attending contacted me regarding their desire to commission my firm for the design of an addition to their church. I knew little about church design, and I knew less about real church master planning. Nevertheless, I did attempt to serve my own church. The final design was a good one, the pastor was satisfied, and I sensed in my heart that I had discovered my calling.

I had known from a young age that I was to be an architect. As a young boy, I really did not know why. But as I had grown in my walk with the Lord, the picture had become clearer. God had planted a desire in my heart to serve the church. I continued to grow in this area of expertise as a church planner, church consultant, church master planner and church architect. My arena of influence grew as churches within my city and churches from other areas began to contact my firm regarding church design.

THE GROWTH OF THE FIRM

I have practiced architecture as a principal since 1979 when I graduated from Virginia Tech. I was a co-founder and managing partner of a local firm from 1980 - 1989. The Lord then directed me to open a new independent architectural company exclusively for the purpose of serving the local church.

I then established the architectural design firm of Barnes Design Group, P. C., Architects/Planners for the purpose of providing complete and comprehensive architectural and engineering services for all types of projects, but most exclusively, specialized services for the local church.

Though Barnes Design Group experienced extensive growth in commercial, industrial, residential and institutional projects, the heart and passion of the firm continued to be in the area of church design. Over the past 15 years, the firm has established itself as a progressive company with an expertise in church consulting, church design and master planning. The firm also has a strong background in renovation, alteration and adaptive reuse projects for the local church.

Ultimately the company's vision for church consulting and planning culminated with the establishment of the following vision and mission statement:

VISION AND MISSION STATEMENT

Corporate Vision
Our vision statement defines our direction and ultimate destination.

Barnes Design Group, P.C., will become a leader in architecture, master planning and vision casting by providing innovative architectural design services of excellence.

In fulfilling this vision, we will work together to...

> Educate and train a dedicated team of architectural, design, master planning, liturgical consulting and 3-D graphics professionals

> Engage in strong strategic partnerships with high-quality contractors, engineers, consultants and other design professionals

> Expand our regional reputation for providing dedicated and quality services to area businesses, corporations, and local churches

> Establish a national reputation for excellence in church master planning and design services for local churches

> Endeavor to become the nation's leading resource for church master planning and design education for church, architectural and construction professionals

Corporate Mission
Our mission statement defines how we corporately plan to fulfill our vision.

Our mission is to expand the ministry of Barnes Design Group to churches while consistently exceeding our clients' hopes and expectations by . . .

> Providing excellence in architectural and design services

> Providing excellence in church master planning services

> Forming a group of creative innovative architects, with a strong sense of mission, bound together in unity and integrity

> Applying the company's "Core Values" every day in all business activities

> Committing to assist our clients in achieving their hopes and dreams

SUMMARY

Our prayer is that God will help us continue to serve Him in the church community as we continually embrace the stated vision and mission statements above. By giving Him the glory in all things and by earnestly serving Him, we believe that we can fulfill our God-given mission. While on this ministry mission, we wholeheartedly embrace the following core values.

CORE VALUES

Our core values represent the things that we value most, both individually and as an organization.

1 > God-Centered. We believe that God is the Creator of all things and for our company to reach its full potential we must operate according to Biblical principles, values and guidelines.

2 > Accountability. We believe that personal and corporate accountability is foundational for long-term success and should exist at every level of our organization.

3 > Excellence. We believe that excellence is required by God and inspires and motivates others to perform at their highest level.

4 > Prayer. We believe that prayer releases the power of God, clarifies vision, cleanses hearts and enables us to maintain intimacy with God and others.

5 > Integrity. We believe that personal and corporate integrity is essential for establishing and maintaining trust-based relationships.

6 > People. We believe that people matter most to God and should matter most to our organization.

7 > Vision. We believe that we are called by God to use our architectural and planning abilities to help our clients clarify and fulfill their vision of the future.

8 > Creativity. We believe that creativity is a gift of God and a foundational step in generating new ideas, finding innovative solutions and producing award-winning designs.

9 > Partnerships. We believe architecture is a cooperative effort and that strategic partnerships with individuals, organizations and clients are necessary for success in the marketplace.

10 > Teamwork. We believe that teamwork produces exceptional results and occurs best in an environment of interdependence, trust and cooperation.■

CHURCH ARCHITECTURE
Professional Service, Ministry or Both?

A FIRM WITH A MISSION
"A Christian firm with a Christian perspective, specializing in church design."

This is an interesting subtitle for this architectural firm in Virginia Beach, Virginia. The firm's specialty is in providing architectural services for a variety of church and church-related clients. However, we are not just any architectural firm. This is a firm with a mission, as God has helped form our directives and build the company.

...SPECIALIZED ARCHITECTURAL DESIGN, MASTER PLANNING SERVICES, 3-D COMPUTER MODELING AND VISION CASTING FOR THE LOCAL CHURCH.

Barnes Design Group, P.C., has created a unique niche in the architectural community — specialized architectural design, master planning services, 3-D computer modeling and vision casting for the local church.

It has always been our goal to have God develop our business plan. Our desire is for God to utilize our professional services for His glory. Though we have provided architectural services on a variety of school projects, residential projects, shopping centers and office buildings over the last twenty years, approximately 95% of our current services are provided directly for churches and church clients.

Barnes Design Group, P.C., has provided architectural services for nearly 300 church commissions. This includes a variety of church projects locally in Virginia as well as churches located in North Carolina, Pennsylvania, Ohio and New Jersey.

In our early years, we developed and explored this architectural profession as a professional service primarily to our corporate and commercial clients. We sought to provide the highest level of professional design services, and we worked hard on the construction drawings used to construct our projects. We viewed our services as a business only, and we did not really view our business as a potential ministry that could be used by God in His kingdom.

However, as we grew and developed professionally and spiritually, we began to explore our work in terms of "architecture as a ministry." Let me briefly explain what I mean.

THE RE-BIRTH OF THE FIRM

My practice of architecture was initially established in 1979 and at that time primarily involved commercial work and overseas government contracts. In the early 80's, I became very serious regarding my relationship with the Lord Jesus Christ. I had been saved as a young boy and therefore knew Jesus as my Savior. However, I did not really know Him as the Lord over my life, the Lord over my finances, the Lord of my family and my business.

However, in the early 80's, I committed my all (including my architectural business) to Him. It was a new experience for me as an architect. We not only gave the company to the Lord, but we seriously began to ask Him to anoint our work and our service. We asked God to give us wisdom. We needed wisdom to run the business, wisdom to find the right clients and the wisdom to know how God would have us lead the local church, which was our newly-found client.

It was at that time when I began to experience the Lord's unique blessing to our venture. He began adding to our business daily. The firm began to grow and we began to experience His direction. It was also at that time that I sensed the Lord direct us specifically into the arena of "church architecture." Our response was to seek His will and pray that the Lord would give us direction to establish our firm as a company that would provide services to the local church as a ministry unto Him.

What was once viewed as only a business and a professional service became a richly blessed ministry that God began to use to grow and lead His local churches. Our wisdom regarding church design began to grow. God began to lead young architects to join the firm and to join arms within this ministry of church architecture. What was once only an idea became a reality as the firm expanded to serve the church in various capacities.

Over the next several years, the Lord did bless the company, give the firm wisdom and establish us in the area of church design and consulting. Barnes Design Group is now viewed in the community as a church specialist and provides services for a variety of church related projects. We have completed the designs of many worship facilities with seating ranging between 500 and 10,000 people. Barnes Design Group was recently commissioned for a 50,000-seat sanctuary located in Madras, India. The firm now provides architectural services for new sanctuaries, additions to existing sanctuaries as well as Christian education buildings, family life centers, social halls and Christian schools.

Barnes Design Group has expanded its professional architectural services in order to meet the needs of a variety of church building types. The firm recently completed the construction drawings on Calvary Academy Middle School. This is a new six million-dollar, beautiful Christian school in Norfolk, Virginia. It is a state-of-the-art Christian Middle School that complements the three million-dollar Christian elementary school and the two million-dollar gym, which we completed a few years ago.

Barnes Design Group not only designs new facilities but also specializes in adaptive reuse of existing facilities. Approximately 40% of the current workload is renovation projects of existing church facilities or additions to existing buildings. The company recently completed renovation drawings for the Princess Anne Plaza Baptist Church elementary school and sanctuary building located in Virginia Beach, Virginia. Reverend Ronald Lee, Pastor of Princess Anne Plaza Baptist Church has the following to say, "Michael Barnes and his company have been a joy to work with...I believe he will be a real blessing to you as he was to us."

MICHAEL BARNES AND HIS COMPANY HAVE BEEN A JOY TO WORK WITH...I BELIEVE HE WILL BE A REAL BLESSING TO YOU AS HE WAS TO US.

THE IMPORTANCE OF SPIRITUAL VISION

We believe that most any architect can design the specific details and structural components that are incorporated into any particular type of building. However, we specialize in the complete long-range master planning encompassing ministry and building needs of the entire church. When we first meet with a church, we discuss short-term needs, long term needs, future growth and the vision of the pastor and leadership team.

We strongly believe that God will bestow upon the Pastor and his team the 'vision' for the church. It is our mission to explore this vision to the point that we, too, fully understand that which God has given to the church. It is then our objective to communicate visually on paper the vision the pastor has for the local church. If we can ultimately and intimately understand the vision that God has given to the church through the local pastor, we are in a better position to assist in creating a design that is conducive and responsive to that vision.

We understand that the local church is not the building itself. We also understand that the ministry of the local church is not the physical facility either. The ministry of the local church is reaching out and touching other lives for Jesus Christ. However, many ministries need the physical facilities we provide in order to be most efficient in accomplishing those objectives. It is in the providing of these physical facilities to house the ministry of the local church whereby we believe the architect's role actually shifts. He should no longer be providing professional services only. He enters into the arena of spiritual ministry as he assists the local pastor in the ministry of the kingdom.

Within his ministry role, the church architect should be intimately involved in the vision casting of the pastor's Godly vision. The church architect's major role is in the capturing of this vision and in the communication of such vision to the congregation. The church architect becomes the "vision caster." Concerning the vision that God gives His people, we are quick to direct our clients to the various scriptures in the Holy Bible pertaining to building and to vision. The following is just a couple of the many scriptures concerning building found in the Holy Bible. We will more fully discuss Biblical and Spiritual applications to building and planning in Chapter 3 titled "The Spiritual Aspects of Building." The scriptures are clear regarding God's impartation of vision and our responsibility to rise up and build.

WHERE THERE IS NO VISION, THE PEOPLE PERISH...
— PROVERBS 29:18

WE SHOULD MAKE PLANS...COUNTING ON GOD TO DIRECT US.
— PROVERBS 16:9

The church architect not only serves as a "vision caster" for the church but also assists the church's leadership in establishing and reviewing their short-term needs and long-term growth projections. The design of the initial structure or any immediate structure must work in harmony with the long-range master planning. The actual master plan may consist of several phases which may be built over a 5-, 10-, or 20-year period. Full master plan design should always be incorporated into the services provided by the church architect.

Barnes Design Group has a passion for Kingdom design. We have extensively studied the Old Testament and have found it rich in Godly wisdom concerning master planning projects. The scriptures clearly teach that Moses had a specific God-given plan for the tabernacle in the wilderness. Noah had specific architectural plans and material specifications for the building of the great ark. And David turned to Solomon before his death and said, "Here are the plans that the Holy Spirit gave me in my mind." Moses, Noah and David represent real true-life examples of leaders in the building process that sought the Lord's direction and received it. We will discuss this further in another chapter.

The architect must work closely with the building committee and/or leadership of the church whereby he can grasp the vision the pastor has for his people. He must be in 'one accord' with the church client he is serving. The architect, as well as the building committee, must be sensitive to God's direction through the design process. We are not designing a church in our back office in order to come to a building committee meeting and hard sell the design product. This is what often happens in the design process.

On the contrary, the architect should meet with the church, meet with the pastor, return to his office and design the project, being sensitive to the needs of the church and the vision that the pastor has communicated to the design team. We believe that ultimately, as the church reviews the work of the architect that is sensitive toward Kingdom design, the building committee will ultimately come to this position....

"It feels good to us and it feels good to the Holy Spirit."

This happens many times on our projects. It is at that time we know we are truly in God's will and are providing a ministry to the Body of Christ and for his Kingdom. Prayer is a key factor in assisting the local church reach its objectives during the design process. An understanding of the pastor's vision, soaked in daily prayer by the architect that is sensitive to the Spirit of God, is paramount in this 'architecture as a ministry' concept.

"

FOR WHO WOULD **BEGIN CONSTRUCTION OF A BUILDING** WITHOUT FIRST GETTING ESTIMATES....
— LUKE 14:28

"

A beautiful design outside of the pastor's vision, without prayer or direction from God, is no more than simple lines on a sheet of paper communicating empty concepts of nothingness. This is really useless in God's kingdom. But architectural services, when viewed and provided as a ministry, can be used by God in many ways. It will bring about a solution to any church's problem. It will also bring Him glory in the process.

The church architect must not only provide good master planning and site design but should also have experience preparing designs that meet ministry requirements within established budget guidelines.

It is important to us, and we believe it is important to God, that the architect correctly identifies the accurate construction cost early in the building program. He must also be accountable to this budget as he completes the construction drawings. Buildings must be designed within established budget guidelines that complement and integrate well with existing facilities and are aesthetically pleasing, high quality and functional. It is a unique ministry to assist the local church in establishing an appropriate budget and then to design an appropriate solution that meets this initial budget. Too often, architects have not concerned themselves about the project budget. It is then a sad time for the local church when they experience construction cost over-runs and budget nightmares. If the budget is not carefully established and followed, the final debt service of the bank can often ruin a local ministry and drive the pastor far from his 'calling.' Ministry ceases to happen and the church loses ground to the enemy of men's souls. We will delve deeper into the financial aspects of planning in Chapter 11, "Financial Considerations."

A BEAUTIFUL DESIGN OUTSIDE OF THE PASTOR'S VISION, WITHOUT PRAYER OR DIRECTION FROM GOD, IS NO MORE THAN SIMPLE LINES ON A SHEET OF PAPER COMMUNICATING EMPTY CONCEPTS OF NOTHINGNESS.

SUMMARY

By approaching church architecture as a ministry to the Kingdom of God, we have been blessed and are now a strong 25-year-old, energetic, Christian, full-service architectural design firm that bases its business on 12 key business principals of the scriptures. We have established 'Key Business Principles' which have helped govern our company and daily walk. These key business principles were established years ago to help provide the firm with a strong foundation.

KEY BUSINESS PRINCIPLES

"To do justice in the marketplace."
— Micah 6:8

Our key business principles provide guidance and direction for our daily decision-making and working environment.

1 > We consider ourselves as stewards, not owners, and willingly submit ourselves to the Godly counsel of our church leaders, Christian business associates and governmental authorities.

2 > We will operate as life-partners, and work together to seek God's guidance and direction in all important business decisions.

3 > We trust God for the ability to make wise financial decisions so that we may experience the blessings of financial freedom that come from owning a debt-free business.

4 > We will always seek to hire staff members that share our passion for God, compassion for people and vision for the marketplace.

5 > We believe that Barnes Design Group is a ministry, and that we should seek to serve the people that God leads our way and help them reach their God-given potential.

6 > We fully acknowledge that the results we achieve are God's grace gifts to us, and are neither deserved nor earned through purely human means.

7 > We will do our best to keep our commitments to God, self and others.

8 > We believe in resolving all conflicts in a way that glorifies God and values others.

9 > We will pray in faith for God's blessings and believe together that He will continually enlarge our territory, bless us with His presence and protect us from evil (I Chronicles 4:10).

10 > We will do our best to set an example of excellence in everything we say and do.

11 > We are committed to helping instill these principles into the lives of our family, friends and business associates.

12 > We accept the Bible as the ultimate authority for all matters of personal faith and business practice.

We live by these twelve principles. We work our business, day to day, based on these principles. Since we believe that this business is a ministry, we approach all we do from this spiritual and Biblical foundation.

In summary, our approach to church design is ministry-based and Spirit-directed. This has grown out of a desire to use our professional expertise to serve God and His local church.

Church design is a combination of efforts of the entire team consisting of the following:

1 > Pastor
2 > Leadership team
3 > Building committee
4 > Architect

The entire team must be working together and praying together regarding God's ultimate will for the church. If the architect is not sensitive and aware of the fact that the design process is a spiritual process, the team is weakened. The church architect must be open to the hand of God within the process. We pray for His direction. We want His thumbprint upon each one of our projects.

God will direct us.

We desire it and we are open to His direction.

Can professional architectural services be a ministry to lead the local church and to give Him the glory?

Yes it can, and yes it is.

We have experienced it and you can too.▪

WHAT IS CHURCH PLANNING?

And Why You Need It!

2

THE BUILDING COMMITTEE'S FIRST MEETING

The setting of the event is nearly always the same. Allow me to describe it to you. Four or five men with as many women are sitting in a living room drinking coffee. They are all faithful members of the 'First Church of their Local City.' They are also friends gathered for a distinct purpose. They are members of the church's building committee. They begin by sharing stories of the previous Sunday morning's service. They sip their coffee and wait patiently for the rest of the building committee to arrive.

...SPATIAL NEEDS FOR THEIR GROWING MINISTRIES.

The starting time was 7:00 p.m. and finally by 7:20 or so, all of the members have arrived. The pastor opens up in prayer and they begin their meeting by discussing one of their most pressing needs of the church spatial needs for their growing ministries.

Often, a local church may outgrow their worship space. Often a growing church outgrows their Christian education facilities. Occasionally, the church needs a family life center for a growing youth ministry. Or perhaps they are a new church plant and need to build their very first facility to house this new ministry.

Nevertheless, all of the building committee members have met with the objective of addressing and solving their spatial problem. Some may even be involved in the construction industry, working for a contractor during the week. However, few if any have professional expertise in the evaluation of spatial problems or experience in the professional design of a church master plan.

After many hours and sometimes many different building committee meetings, the members can often become distraught in the process. The understanding of spatial needs, the evaluation of church growth, the understanding of church architecture and the construction costing of appropriate structures are well beyond the average committee's experience. It is not that the local church cannot review their needs and even suggest some appropriate solutions to their problem. It is that they usually do not have the depth of experience needed for a complete evaluation of design approaches and for the study of the alternatives.

CHURCH COMMITTEES ARE OFTEN **UNABLE TO IDENTIFY AND ADDRESS** THE POTENTIAL CHALLENGES THAT THE **CHURCH MAY FACE** DURING THE NEXT 5, 10 OR **EVEN 20** YEARS.

Most church committees can certainly identify the current most pressing challenges of their present situation. However, they are often unable to identify and address the potential challenges that the church may face during the next 5, 10 or even 20 years. In fact, we have often worked with churches and reviewed past design solutions whereby the original design professional considered only the pressing present problem and did not consider the future growth of the church.

In light of the potential future needs of a local church, many times the most likely design solution of the present challenge is inappropriate. Building additions may be located in the wrong location, parking may be designed in the way of a future building and heating or electrical systems may be under-designed. This can result in wasted money and the removal of past building systems in order to meet future needs.

A successful master plan always addresses the church's current challenges, as well as the projected future needs of that local church. It is not uncommon for appropriate church master planning to identify and respond to the following issues:

> Immediate needs and challenges of the church
> Projected needs and challenges in 5 years
> Projected needs and challenges in 10 years
> Projected needs and challenges in 15 years
> Projected needs and challenges in 20 years

WHAT IS A MASTER PLAN?

Now that we have addressed the need for successful master planning for the local church, let's define exactly what a church master plan really is.

THE DEFINITION OF "MASTER PLANNING"
A church master plan is a concise, written-out and defined declaration of the church's tentative assumptions about God's will for their church life, embracing directives for the guidance of the church's physical facilities *and* embracing the directives for the church's organizational planning — resulting in actual blueprints for the church's future growth.

It is the responsibility of the church planner and architect to assist the church in defining the goals and objectives of the master plan. The master plan will assist in the formulation of the following:

> Future spiritual goals
> Future physical goals
> Formulation of the vision
> Design directives for the planning
> Renderings to visually communicate the architectural solution to the problem

STARTING THE MASTER PLAN PROCESS...

The architect will first assist the client with the problem definition. It is very important to define carefully the exact challenge that the church is currently facing in their building project. The architect is to assist the church with this process by providing the following documents for the church's review, prior to starting the final design drawings.

Goals and Objectives Statement

This document provides a clear and concise definition of the wishes and the vision which the Pastor and his leadership has from God. This will determine and document the clear objectives, which will ultimately guide the architect in the formulation of a master plan design blueprint for the church. This document will define the vision and directives of the church's program for the present time as well as define the vision and directives for the 5, 10, 15 or 20-year program as well. One of the most important elements of the entire master planning process is this actual goal and objective statement, as it becomes foundational in the parameters of the ultimate design solution.

Spatial Square Footage Analysis

Once the goals and objectives of the church have been established and defined, the architect can now ascertain the exact spaces required to meet the needs of the current and future challenges. This document should list each and every space, responding to the specific needs of the church. The number of people required by the church in each space can further define the space requirements. The competent and experienced church planner has no problem translating the people count of each space into final square footages. Once the total square footage has been established for each required space, the total square footage of the proposed project can be established by the careful evaluation of the following support spaces:

> Heating and cooling equipment rooms
> Electrical rooms
> Required exit halls
> Space taken up by exterior and interior walls
> Janitor closets and storage rooms

Opinion of Construction Cost

Once the square footage of the entire project has been fully established, the architect can establish the appropriate and expected construction cost of the project. In many situations, the final construction cost is not established until the complete design and construction drawings have been completed. However, it is important to fully consider the cost of the project prior to starting any design solution drawings for the client. Not only is this good planning, but it is Biblical as well. An experienced church architect and planner can translate the 'Spatial Square Foot Analysis' into an 'Opinion of Construction Cost' without a tremendous effort. This early cost can help the church determine if they can afford those spaces they have identified in this early master plan process without expending great sums of fees.

THE MASTER PLAN DESIGN PROCESS

Once these three master planning documents have been completed by the architect and approved by the church's leadership, the architect is in a position to start the final master planning design documents for the church's review. Once the goals and objectives and the square footage analysis has been successfully evaluated by the architect and their church client, the design is a simple reflection and response to the parameters already set, documented and approved.

The architect will begin the site design, floor plan design and the building elevation design. The proposed design solutions, when reviewed, should always be compared to the pre-planning documents already completed. We refer to this as architectural design accountability.

The typical architectural design is represented and evaluated to the client by site plans, floor plans and building elevations. Allow me to describe each of these below.

Site Plan

The site plan must allow for the building placement and parking arrangement for the current church needs, as well as reflect the future needs which have been identified. The master site plan may reflect many phases of the building program. It is not unusual for the site plan to identify several phases reflecting current needs and projected future needs. These different phases of the plan must work together and complement one another. The site plan must illustrate a balance between the building footprint and parking throughout each phase of the plan. This required ratio between building size and parking is most always dictated by the city's comprehensive zoning requirements.

Floor Plan

The floor plan of the project will reflect the needs and the actual square footages already determined and documented in the prior analysis. The floor plan illustrates the building form and the relationships between the various spaces. It will lay out the building flow and the size and shape of all of the spaces. The relationships between the interior spaces and the exterior spaces are also defined. Often the floor plan will identify phases for the complete building program.

Building Elevations

The building design elevations (what the building looks like from the exterior) will also be developed for the review of the church at this time. Studies of exterior building materials and their composition into the whole building will be reflected in these drawings. The architect will prepare detail elevation drawings of all four sides of the building for the church's review. Often these will be colored and rendered to make them more understandable to the client. Though architects are very adept in visualizing the entire building design from these building elevation drawings, 3-D renderings are best utilized to fully communicate the design approach to a client.

THE MASTER PLAN COMPUTER 3-D RENDERINGS & ANIMATIONS

Once the church leadership has approved the site plan, floor plans, elevations and the final phasing of the project, the architect will reflect all of these design particulars in a final computer 3-D rendering. This rendering will be created using correct material textures and colors in order to create a realistic photo-like final rendering of the project. This can best communicate to the church the final design solution for the need at hand.

3-D DIGITAL MODELING IS A POWERFUL COMPUTER PROCESS THAT ALLOWS THE ARCHITECT TO CREATE LIFELIKE IMAGES OF THE FINISHED PRODUCT.

In our experience, it is often the 3-D photo realistic computer renderings that most effectively communicate the vision to the church. This rendering can utilize the exact background of the site location and the landscaping that are located around the existing building. We will often photograph several specifics of the existing buildings or site and scan the images into the computer. This will create a real life-like final rendition that best communicates the 'real-ness' of the rendering to the client.

In fact, several years back, we began to request from our church clients actual photographs of the pastors, leadership, members and even children. We scan these images into the computer and place them into the 3-D computer renderings. Obviously, the photographs could not look staged. They would need to be action photos. We would use group photos of people talking or walking around the building. We could then place these action photos into the final rendering creating the impression that the rendering was in fact a final photo of the project. Sun angles would reflect the actual site. The background and sky conditions would indicate a very realistic approach to this rendering.

Sometimes we present these to the church body as final renderings mounted and framed. However, other times we have used a PowerPoint presentation to present our ideas and concepts, followed with a large format PowerPoint presentation of the renderings themselves. This can be most impressive and effective in communicating "the vision."

It is important to realize that we are not proposing that the architect utilize high-tech computer photo-realistic 3-D renderings for the sake of using high-tech approaches to the design process. On the contrary, we see this new software as an opportunity to better serve our church clients in the vision casting of the early phases of the project. The pastor may have a vision of the project and the architect may even buy into the vision and understand the goals and objectives as well. But unless the church architect can realistically communicate this vision to the church body with passion, his work is useless.

We want to be effective in our artistic and visual representation of the final architectural solution. The 3-D computer renderings offer us that opportunity to best serve our church client and cast the final vision to their church. Barnes Design Group utilizes both 3-D computer-modeled renderings (which are similar to still photographs), as well as 3-D computer animation to cast the vision of the design to the church. 3-D digital modeling is a powerful computer process that allows the architect to create lifelike images of the finished product. Computer wire frames are drawn using computer modeling programs that create various shapes and solids of the geometry of the architect's design.

Then colors and textures are 'mapped' onto the shapes and solids to depict the various building materials such as brick, glass or metal. Then environmental elements are added such as sky, trees, cars and people.

THE
VISION

Lastly, we add virtual 'lights' to the computer scene to illuminate the virtual model as if it were a sunny day or perhaps in the evening with the building all lit up. The end result is a 'realistic rendering' of the intended design that looks very much like a photograph of the final product.

Never before has such a powerful communication tool been available to the architectural client. Barnes Design Group utilizes this tool, providing it as an 'in-house' service. With a computer-generated rendering, the client can get a good look at their building before it's ever built. The computer-generated rendering goes a long way in casting the vision of the new building to others. Even financial institutions that are often involved in the financing of a project can better grasp the intended design by viewing a computer-modeled rendering. The renderings are the vehicle for communicating the vision of the project to the congregation as parishioners can see what they are investing in.

There are actually two different types of 3-D renderings. Above we have discussed the 'still renderings' which are snapshots of the building and a representation of its surrounding environment. Our still renderings are available in digital format in almost any size and can be used on pamphlets, web pages, PowerPoint presentations and are often printed on large boards and framed to hang on the walls of the church. However, a second type of 3-D rendering is the 3-D animation. This is a miniature movie of the entire building usually lasting 4-5 minutes in duration.

This animation is often combined with music and other thematic elements like scripture selections. The 3-D animations are actually very similar to walking around the final building with a video camera in your hand. They are a powerful complement to fund-raising programs and vision casting and can be very moving both emotionally and spiritually.

While many firms who offer 3-D rendering services 'outsource' or hire another company to produce them, Barnes Design Group feels that it is such an important part of the vision casting to churches, that we produce them all in-house. That means that our staff is intimately involved in the production process during the design so that the final product of the 3-D renderings, as well as the animations, 'fit' the client or the congregation.

It is the pastor's heartbeat and vision that we wish to convey to the church. We do this best by using state-of-the-art computer software that produces 3-D photo-realism in our computer renderings and computer animations work.

Does it really convey the vision effectively?

Consider the following comments we most often hear from the parishioners after a church has reviewed such 3-D renderings of the proposed project for the first time:

These renderings have blessed our many church clients and can bless your church as well.

"

I COULD REALLY SEE US WORSHIPPING IN THAT FACILITY. I CAN REALLY VISUALIZE IT.

IT SEEMS SO REAL WITH OUR PASTOR STANDING OUT FRONT AND ALL… ALMOST JUST LIKE A PHOTOGRAPH.

WE HAVE TALKED ABOUT THIS FOR SO LONG NOW, I ALMOST BEGAN TO FEEL LIKE WE WOULD NEVER ACCOMPLISH WHAT GOD HAD FOR US. BUT JUST LOOKING AT THAT COMPUTER RENDERING, MAKES ME FEEL LIKE WE HAVE ALREADY ACCOMPLISHED IT. WITH GOD'S HELP, WE CAN BUILD IT.

"

ADVANTAGES OF HAVING A MASTER PLAN

There are various advantages of creating a master plan for the church. Though a complete master plan, which addresses current and future needs of the church, often takes more time than merely solving the present needs only, the benefits of such a master plan are numerous. Let's review some of the most important benefits of a church master plan:

Management Tool

One of the most obvious benefits of a completed master plan is that it provides a valuable management tool for the church's leadership. The church leadership will now have a complete documentation of their facility needs for the present as well as for the future. They will understand the building size requirements, and they will have a complete cost accounting of each phase. This will allow the leadership to provide financial cost planning in order for the church to reach their building needs.

Ministry Reflection

The master plan also provides a visual representation of the church leadership's vision for the congregation. The site plan, floor plans and the 3-D photo-like renderings illustrate the vision of the church in truly amazing ways. We understand that the building is not the church. We understand that the church is the people and the vision of the church represents the ministry directives that God has laid on the hearts of the leadership. Nevertheless, in this culture and climate, ministry often requires the housing of a church building, and the master plan documents best reflect this ministry expansion and church vision.

Congregational Focus

The master plan is often presented to the entire congregation for approval. We will often mount all of these documents on large boards and have them framed behind glass for display. These documents are then displayed in a central area like the church's lobby. The congregation is reminded time and time again regarding the church leadership's vision, goals, dreams and objectives as they review these design documents on display. This provides focus for the church as they can now easily understand the vision and support it.

Communication to Visitors

The pastor or the church architect presents the final master plan drawings when they are complete. The drawings can then be displayed in the central lobby. This can establish a clear focus for the parishioners that are present. However, the new visitors arriving at the church weeks later may not understand the vision of the church. Though the pastor cannot take every Sunday morning to review the vision, the master plan design documents can be displayed each and every Sunday for visitors to review at their leisure. The communication of the church's vision to the first-time visitor can make the difference between the visitor coming back the next Sunday or visiting another church.

NOTE: The limitations of your church will be identified by your visitors. If the church is experiencing problems with facilities, believe me, a visitor will readily perceive them. If there are real limitations with your physical facilities that are inhibiting your church from experiencing real growth, you must clearly respond to these factors by identifying them and solving these challenges. The church is then in a better position to be proactive by communicating these limitations and your response to such limitations in a complete master plan design.

A clear, concise master plan will bless your church for years to come. The small cost of having a professional church architect provide your church with these master planning services will be ultimately offset by the advantages of your parishioners understanding and buying into your vision. People will financially support that which is clear, concise and understandable. Your vision should be cast with clarity and confidence.

The church architect must focus on real needs, real solutions and relate the solution to the actual mission of the church as defined by the pastor and his leadership team. The master plan must be presented in a positive and enthusiastic manner mixed with excitement and inspiration. If presented in this way, the church can better understand the vision, the mission and the direction that God is leading the pastor. God can prosper this type of plan and He does.

"He will prosper us; therefore we His servants will arise and build…"
— Nehemiah 2:20

SYMPTOMS OF NOT HAVING A MASTER PLAN

Just as there are advantages of using a master plan, there are some real disadvantages to a church that does not effectively utilize a master plan to assist in their church planning and growth stage.

Lack of Management Direction

Just as a master plan becomes an effective management tool as discussed above, the lack of a master plan can be a poor reflection of a church management/leadership team without direction. People need direction and vision. The pastor can verbally address the vision. He can communicate the church's intentions regarding the expansion of their facilities. However, a verbal discussion of the vision cannot provide the direction that a complete master plan can provide. Without clear direction, there is absolutely no context within the church for proper God-directed decision making regarding the church's growth and their response to such growth.

Lack of Apparent Vision

The pastor may have a strong God-directed vision for the church. He may have even discussed it during certain sermons or during business meetings. However, without some type of strong visual representation of his vision, as it relates to the physical facilities and the church's growth, the people may or may not really sense the reality of the goals and dreams. I call this symptom the 'lack of apparent vision.' I have had many pastors share with me their church vision and how they have communicated it with their congregation. However, I have discovered in many church meetings that their people have not had a clear understanding of the pastor's vision to date. A pastoral leadership team, though strong, may appear weak if there is a perceived lack of communicated vision to the church.

Lack of Focus

If the pastor's dreams, vision, goals and objectives are not clearly documented and presented in an understandable form to the church, the church ultimately will lose focus. They lose grasp of their mission and how their facilities can assist them in accomplishing ministry goals. A lack of ministry focus in a church can create difficulties in the body. Without a clear focus of vision, non-leaders often can begin communicating their own false visions for their church. They may begin with their friends or closest companions. These 'mini-false-visions' may not be in line with the pastor's God-given vision. In fact, many times these false-visions perpetuated by leader-wannabes are diametrically opposed to the God-given vision. This lack of focus resulting in false vision statements can produce tension, confusion, frustration and trouble.

Potential Funding Problems

Unclear goals and objectives or confusing vision and ministry statements can ultimately create a nightmare of funding problems for the church. People need to believe in the vision in order to financially support it. People wish to be led by an exciting visionary. Without a clear master plan of growth, donors just won't give to a program. When there is no need and when there is no plan, people in the church will not give effectively. The growing church can quickly outgrow...

> Physical facilities
> Office staffing
> Pastoral staffing
> Available operating funds
> Available building funds

Without a clear vision, the church can be left unprepared for growth. They will often experience a lack of appropriate funding for the church needs as listed above. A ministry cannot grow without proper funding, and proper funding is difficult to establish with an unclear vision. A properly executed and prepared master plan can establish a pastor's vision and assist in such funding.

SUMMARY

It is important to fully establish ministry directives and God-given vision for ministry. I understand that the architect is not the only instrument used by God to establish such vision directive. However, the church architect is the instrument that God can use to effectively communicate the vision (regarding building or expansion) to the church.

The qualified professional "Christian" church architect can be used by God in the appropriate visual communication of the pastoral vision to the people. The scriptures tell us that without a vision, the people perish. But as we have discussed above, the pastor can have a vision that has been communicated to him from God. But if that vision is not appropriately communicated to the people in such a visual way that the vision can be grasped by the typical church parishioner, the vision provides no leadership or inspiration.

The architect can provide an extremely valuable service by working together with the church team to establish a comprehensive master plan that is communicated by a computer generated 3-D rendering. In this way, God can richly bless the vision that he has given to the pastor of the church. The church can rise to the occasion by embracing the God-given vision and supporting the building programs as illustrated by the master plan.

The master plan is perhaps the greatest tool available to us to communicate the entire pastoral vision to the local church body today.■

THE SPIRITUAL ASPECTS OF CHURCH BUILDING 3
Noah, Moses and Solomon

NOT BY MIGHT...

I overheard an individual the other day make the following statement, "I attend the church located at 17th Street and Atlantic Boulevard near the oceanfront."

What this person was actually stating was his affiliation with a local congregation of God's universal church. However, it is not unusual for us, in today's society and culture, to refer to the 'church' as different buildings located throughout the city on different streets. We often refer to different churches by referring to their physical characteristics such as churches

IN REALITY, THESE STRUCTURES ARE NOT THE 'CHURCH' AT ALL.

with large steeples or churches with small steeples. There are churches with large spires that seat 5,000 people and there are small missionary outreach churches that seat only a few hundred.

In reality, these structures are not the 'church' at all. The church of Jesus Christ is not the sanctuary nor is it the fellowship hall or classrooms that we so readily occupy and refer to as the 'church.' The buildings are not the real church. We understand that God's Spirit does not dwell within the walls of the physical sanctuary. At one time, His spirit did dwell within a physical structure, as it inhabited the Holy of Holies. However, Jesus Christ, His birth, death and resurrection changed all of that.

You might recall, it was the tearing of the veil in the temple that occurred during the crucifixion of Jesus at His death. The veil had historically separated the Holy of Holies from the rest of the temple. It was the tearing of the veil in the temple that released God from the inner-sanctum of a building into the sanctuary of our own hearts. It was a work of Jesus Christ. In today's society, the Church is the body of Jesus Christ made up of individuals who have accepted Him into their hearts. God now "tabernacles," or lives, in our spirit rather than a physical structure.

The Word of God is very clear in defining the location of the dwelling of God's Holy Spirit. This truth is best reflected in the following verses:

"

GOD DOESN'T LIVE IN TEMPLES MADE BY HUMAN HANDS.
— ACTS 17:24

DON'T YOU REALIZE THAT ALL OF YOU TOGETHER ARE THE HOUSE OF GOD AND THAT THE SPIRIT OF GOD LIVES AMONG YOU IN HIS HOUSE.
— I CORINTHIANS 3:16

DO YOU NOT KNOW THAT YOUR BODY IS A TEMPLE OF THE HOLY SPIRIT, WHO IS IN YOU, WHOM YOU HAVE RECEIVED FROM GOD? YOU ARE NOT YOUR OWN.
— I CORINTHIANS 6:19

"

It is Paul that reminds us in I Corinthians 6:19 that our body is the temple of the Holy Spirit. He reminds the body of Christ (or the church in Ephesus) that we are the ones carefully joined together with Christ as parts of a beautiful and constantly growing temple of God. The temple located in Jerusalem no longer contains the Spirit of the God of Abraham. The Spirit's dwelling place is now within our very own hearts.

As we consider church building throughout this book, I am referring to the physical facilities that house the ministries of the local church. There are a variety of church ministries in today's society that are a reflection of the Lord's ministry through us. They are often housed in specific building complexes located on the church's grounds. The following is a brief listing of some of the more apparent ministry needs of the local church:

> Sanctuary space for corporate worship and the preaching of God's word.

> Administrative space for the church's office staff.

> Christian Education space which houses classrooms for teaching the Gospel.

> Family Life Centers which house social events for the church.

The church is the body of believers. In this I am certain.

The early church, as reflected in Acts, met in believers' households as they regularly broke bread, read scriptures, encouraged one another and praised and worshipped God on a regular basis. However, ministry in today's society most often occurs within a physical architecture. Though it is this architecture, the planning of this architecture and the ultimate building of the same that we are concerned of in this particular book, it is important that we do not lose sight of the fact that ultimately the entire process is a spiritual journey.

Consider the following scripture:

> **"**
>
> SO HE SAID TO ME, 'THIS IS THE WORD OF THE LORD TO ZERUBBABEL: NOT BY MIGHT NOR BY POWER, BUT BY MY SPIRIT SAYS THE LORD ALMIGHTY.'
> — ZECHARIAH 4:6
>
> **"**

The Lord is reminding us that in all of our journeys, the process is a spiritual one. The accomplishments that we make, whether it be in the preaching of a sermon or the building of a sanctuary is, "not by might nor by power, but by my Spirit." It is by the Lord's Spirit that we accomplish great things for Him. We are always to remind ourselves that the process is a spiritual one.

It is very easy, in this physical building process, for our perspective to shift from the spiritual to the physical due to the fact that the ultimate product is a physical one and is built with bricks and mortar. Nevertheless, the entire journey from master planning through design to ultimate construction is indeed a very spiritual process that can grow the church deep in Him. This will often occur from the beginning of the design process to the time when the contractor is constructing the building on the site.

THE LORD IS REMINDING US THAT IN ALL OF OUR JOURNEYS, THE PROCESS IS, A SPIRITUAL ONE.

The facilities that we address throughout this book are but tools that encapsulate the actual ministry of the true church. They should be designed to reach the lost. Church buildings are not to be edifices to glorify the church or to establish the architect as a great designer. They are merely buildings to accomplish ministry and in all cases must bring glory to Him.

All architectural church buildings should be designed specifically for ministry. The form and the design of the architecture should reflect the ministry it houses. A building built without a ministry need is really not a church building at all. That type of structure is built by our "might" and by our "power" and typically not by His Spirit. This is not what we want.

All church architectural solutions must be designed with the unchurched in mind. If the goal and objective of the church is to reach the lost and to proclaim the Gospel to the uttermost parts of the earth, then church buildings must ultimately be designed with the objective to accomplish the same. Whether we are designing the interior spaces of Christian education classrooms, the sanctuary chancel that will house the praise and worship team or the worship space where believers corporately gather on a Sunday morning, the design must be accomplished with the unchurched in mind.

NEVERTHELESS, THE ENTIRE JOURNEY FROM MASTER PLANNING THROUGH DESIGN TO ULTIMATE CONSTRUCTION IS INDEED A VERY SPIRITUAL PROCESS THAT CAN GROW THE CHURCH DEEP IN HIM.

We must remind ourselves as architects, church planners and building committee members that the facilities are really not being designed and built to house Christians and add to their physical and mental comfort only. There is nothing wrong with a building that accomplishes some of those objectives and is pleasing to the eye as well. I believe that God expects the church to shine and be an example of Godly excellence in all ways. However, a church that accomplishes physical and artistic goals without adding to needed ministry objectives of the church has indeed drifted from the heartbeat of God.

As we walk through this seemingly "physical" process, we must always remind ourselves of the word the Lord gave to Zerubbabel, which is "not by might nor by power, but by my Spirit."

A TIME TO BUILD

I will never forget when I was praying regarding my architectural firm many years ago. I was a partner with another local architect in Virginia Beach, and we provided architectural services for shopping centers, federal government facilities, local schools, apartments, motels, hotels and churches. However, I began to sense in my heart that God had something else for me to do. As I continued to pray regarding my mission here on earth, a desire began to grow inside of me for serving the local church. There were several times when I felt I was ready to branch out specifically on my own to serve the church world. But the time had not come.

> NOTE: Even in the ministry of Jesus, all things were done according to God's holy time schedule. The Lord walked on the earth until the 'time had fully come.' He preached the Gospel 'when the time had come' and when the 'time had fully come,' he told his disciples 'it was time' for Him to enter Jerusalem.

Several months after I had originally felt compelled to leave my professional firm and branch out in a church-related architectural venture, the Lord spoke to my heart. In His perfect timing, I received a vision while in prayer early one morning. There was no question about the direction. There was absolutely no question regarding my

"

THE DAY FOR BUILDING YOUR WALLS WILL COME, THE DAY FOR EXTENDING YOUR BOUNDARIES.
— MICAH 7:11

"

mission. The Lord showed me a vision of my future. The scripture speaks specifically about God's timing. Consider the following scriptures:

"There is a time for everything, and a season for every activity under heaven: a time to be born and a time to die, a time to plant and a time to uproot, a time to kill and a time to heal, a time to tear down and a time to build..."
— Ecclesiastes 3:1-3

Not only was there a perfect timing for me to start a new company that would be of service to His Kingdom, but there is also a perfect timing for His church to build. We are reminded in Micah 7:11 that the day for building the walls of the church will come. In God's perfect timing, He will provide the vision and plans including the goals and objectives for your building project. When the day for building finally comes, He will provide the finances, for He owns the cattle on a thousand hills. When the day comes for extending your boundaries, the Lord will make it clear.

> Solomon states there is a time for everything and a season for every activity.

> Have you entered into your time?

> Is it your season?

> Are ministries birthing under God's direction at your church where there are no physical facilities to house such ministries?

> Are existing ministries growing to the extent that your boundaries are being increased though your physical facilities cannot bear the strain?

Solomon states there is a time to tear down and a time to build. When working with the local church, I always like to ask them if their time has come. Has the day arrived for the extension of their boundaries? Has the time come to build? God's timing is critical. We might have the right solution and understand the problem. We might have the vision statement and understand our spiritual calling. But if the day has not come, we will be too early and we will be out of step with God's perfect will for our lives.

As a church architect, I stress this spiritual timing issue. I do not want to be involved with the building of a local church if their "time has not come." The building process can be a challenging one, even when the time has come. I am sorry to say that we have had experiences whereby we have struggled and struggled, as a church architect, to assist churches in their building projects. Many times, extensive fees are paid and time is lost. The credibility of the leadership team is reduced and ultimately no church is built.

Unfortunately, many architects' files are full of drawings that have been designed for churches that have never built. Designed...drawn...but never constructed and occupied. My guess is that their time had not fully come.

SPIRITUAL DIRECTIVES

There are many scriptures throughout the Word of God that give us specific directives regarding the building of facilities to house ministries within His Kingdom on earth. It is important that we understand these spiritual directives and that we walk our walk according to these Biblical truths. It is critical that both the leadership team, as well as the architect, not only understand these spiritual directives that are found in scripture but apply them throughout the journey.

Let's consider a few of the scriptural directives that the Lord gives us regarding this spiritual process of building:

UNLESS THE LORD BUILDS THE HOUSE ITS BUILDERS LABOR IN VAIN.
— PSALMS 127:1

1 > Unless the Lord builds...

It's important to understand that the Lord is the master builder. He was the original architect, engineer and master planner of the universe. In fact, He is the master of the universe.

He spoke the world into existence and it became. He spoke the planets and hung the stars in space by His very word. David reminds us in the Psalm that the builders cannot labor effectively unless the Lord builds. Inherent in the verse is a concept of timing and God's will.

We are not to attempt the planning process or the building in our own power. We are to make certain that the Lord is doing the building. It is easy for an architect to pick up a set of drawings, study the building code or review the municipality city ordinances and begin to sense that we are the master builder. We are certainly to understand the typical construction processes and the building code. However, the journey is a spiritual journey. The Lord must build the house. He gives us direction, insight, vision and anointing. This can only be achieved if the architect and the building committee work in unity with the pastor.

2 > God directs us...

"We should make plans...counting on God to direct us."
— Proverbs 16:9

Solomon reminds us that we make the plans. In my earlier days of architecture, we often did the drawings specifically on vellum with lead pencils. Currently, computers with CADD programs accomplish all of our drawings. I have never seen a pen take off drawing, and I have never seen a computer accomplish plans on its own accord.

We make the plans.

The church itself sets the mission statement in accordance with their perception of God's will. The architect assists the church leadership in expressing the goals and visions of the church through written documents. We then design the project by drawing plans to reflect that vision, mission statement, goals and objectives.

However, it is important to remember that we are to count on God to direct us.

Well-written plans, whether they be goals and objective statements or architectural plans, help to commit us to a cause. I have never seen any man of God accomplish anything for the Lord that the Lord did not communicate to him and then he write it out as a plan.

Well-drawn plans reflect God's vision.

Well-thought-out plans reflect the mission of the church.

Well-conceived plans give direction to the church leadership, as well as to the entire body. We make the plans but the direction comes from God.

3 > Vision is critical...

"Where there is no vision the people perish."
— Proverbs 29:18

Vision begins with God. No building project can successfully take place and honor Him without that vision. I believe the vision flows from God to the spiritual leadership of the church, which often is the senior pastor. The vision then flows from the pastor to his leadership and then ultimately to the church architect.

The architect must understand the pastor's vision. This is critical. All too often, plans are drawn by architects that do not reflect the vision God has given to the pastor. People, as sheep, need direction. Vision

I HAVE NEVER SEEN ANY MAN OF GOD ACCOMPLISH ANYTHING FOR THE LORD THAT THE LORD DID NOT COMMUNICATE TO HIM AND THEN HE WRITE IT OUT AS A PLAN.

communicates direction. Without direction there are often very low expectations. And without expectations and faith, the ultimate results are minimal. We have worked with churches like this.

So, what is the meaning of this scripture as it applies to this design process? Vision is direct revelation from God. It is the first stepping stone in the building design process. The original Hebrew word "perish" actually means walking in circles or getting out of hand. It is like disheveled hair.

In paraphrasing, this verse might state the following...

"Where there is no direct spiritual revelation from God regarding His ministry through the local church and ultimately the buildings that will encompass that ministry, the people of that church will never build successfully and will ultimately walk in circles without clear direction of what God would have them do."

Even a successful church architect cannot serve a church where there is no vision.

4 > Estimating is important...

"For who would begin construction of a building without first getting estimates..."
— Luke 14:28

I was recently at a church builder's convention and heard a staggering statistic:

Approximately 80% of churches that build have a common denominator and that common denominator is "over-budget, expensive buildings" with substantial cost overruns. In fact, a common quoted rule of thumb is that 80% of projects run at least 30% over budget. Quite simply, I believe that this is poor stewardship. It is often a poor reflection on the ability of the architect to accomplish that which is being spoken of in Luke chapter 14. God desires for us to count the cost. The Lord Jesus Christ asked the question, "For who would begin the construction of a building without first getting estimates?" We believe that stewardship is not only a spiritual concept, but that the actual application of financial criteria suitable for establishing correct and true budgets and estimates up front is Biblical. It is our responsibility. God desires us to count the cost and we are accountable for that. The architect is accountable for true cost estimating of the building and the church is accountable for true cost accounting of the entire project cost. For actual cost considerations and for a discussion of the difference between construction cost and project cost, please see Chapter 11 on "Financial Considerations," which addresses this entire issue.

We are responsible for accurately counting the cost early in the process before we build, not after the construction drawings are completed. Remember that knowledge of building costs is no good to the church board unless the application of wisdom is applied to it. Godly wisdom is the appropriate application of knowledge, which enables His kingdom to be further established.

APPROPRIATE COST KNOWLEDGE

+

THE APPLICATION OF GODLY WISDOM

=

SUCCESS OF A BUILDING PROJECT.

5 > God cares about the details...

"Carry out the plan in every detail for it is the will of the Lord."
— I Chronicles 17:2

We are to carry out our plans in every detail. One only needs to look at the directives that God gave Noah to understand that God is a God of details. The tabernacle was designed by God and communicated to Moses and he was to build it according to the details. The Lord says to Moses in I Chronicles to carry out the plan in every detail for that is the will of the Lord. What does "in every detail" really mean? I believe it means that we are to prepare designs that reflect ministry requirements. We are to understand the ministry of the church in finite detail so that the buildings that house the ministries will reflect this detail.

I believe carrying out the plan in every detail means that we are to prepare designs within established budgets as we stated above. Budgets are important. Accountability to cost is important, and the Lord will hold us accountable for being good stewards of the money that comes into the local church.

I believe that carrying out the plan in every detail also means that as church architects, we are to prepare designs that compliment and integrate with any existing structures. God is interested in the details. We are to prepare designs that are architecturally and aesthetically pleasing to the eye. Such designs are to be totally functional as well as examples of design excellence. We are to carry out such planning in every detail.

We are to prepare designs that reflect the detail of the vision the Lord has given the church. All plans are to be carried out in details.

6 > He will prosper...

"He will prosper us; therefore we as servants will arise and build..."
— Nehemiah 2:20

God will prosper his people. This is a scriptural truth. As we give, God will pour out His blessings. The scripture teaches "give and it shall be given unto you." This is a universal spiritual truth that is presented throughout the Word of God. I think it is obvious that God will prosper his people. The scripture above says, "He will prosper us."

FINANCES CRIPPLE FEWER CHURCHES THAN THE FEAR OF FINANCES.

However, we must respond to the blessings of the Lord. God's people will be accountable for their response. This scripture says once He prospers us, we as servants must arise.

I believe that arise means exactly what it says. We are to get up and get started. I have had many churches talk to me for years about building. They have the finances, they are looking at the land, but they never arise. Jesus told the crippled man to, "Arise, take your bed and walk." The crippled man could have sat on the bed for weeks talking about the Godly truths and the spiritual direction that the Lord Jesus Christ Himself had given him.

However, it took action on his part and that action was very simple. He was to arise. Finances cripple fewer churches than the fear of finances. I have talked to many churches that have been absolutely crippled by the fear of finances. I believe that God prospers us and we are to arise and build.

7 > Always be strong...

"Be strong and courageous, and do the work. Do not be afraid or discouraged for the Lord, my God is with you. He will not fail you or forsake you until all the work...is finished."
— I Chronicles 28:20

It is important that we are to be strong and courageous. As I stated above, we are also to do the work. We are to arise, take our bed and walk. The above scripture tells us that we are not to be afraid or discouraged. Discouragement often cripples building plans. This scripture reminds us that God is with us.

He will not fail us and he will not forsake us until the work is finished. It is the work of the Lord and we are to do that work with his help. God will do it because he is with us.

Discouragement can often come upon a building committee. I've sat with many leadership committees of a local church and observed them as they discussed their 'discouragements.' The devil will often try to discourage the church, and it often comes in finances or in the fear of finances. Therefore, the Word tells us we are not to be afraid or discouraged for God is with us. He will not fail us or forsake us.

BIBLICAL EXAMPLES OF BUILDING

Now that we have studied the specific scriptural directives regarding building projects, let's look at three important examples of building in the Old Testament. These examples are the Ark of Noah, the Tabernacle of Moses and the Temple of Solomon.

The Ark of Noah...

"But Noah found favor in the eyes of the Lord. This is the account of Noah. Noah was a righteous man, blameless among the people of his time and he walked with God."
— Genesis 6:8-9

"So make yourself an ark of cypress wood; make rooms in it and coat it with pitch inside and out. This is how you are to build it: the ark is to be 450 ft. long, 75 ft. wide and 45 ft. high. Make a roof for it and finish the ark to within 18 in. of the top. Put a door in the side of the ark and make lower middle and upper decks. I am going to bring floodwaters on the earth to destroy all life under the heavens, every creature that has the breath of life in it. Everything on earth will perish but I will establish a covenant with you and you will enter the ark - you and your sons, and your wife and sons' wives with you."
— Genesis 6:14-18

There are several incredible, deep, spiritual truths that can be gleamed out of the "Ark of Noah" account that are directly applicable to building projects today.

To begin with, Noah had no boat building experience. Noah had not built any fishing boats, yachts or cruise vessels up to that point. In fact, we have no way of knowing if Noah even knew what a boat was or how a boat would float upon the waters. To our knowledge, he had absolutely no experience with boat building. It was not by his might or by his power that gave him the qualifications needed to serve God in such a way.

It was not by might or by power, but it was by "His Spirit" that dwelled within Noah. The verse above tells us that Noah found favor in the eyes of the Lord, was a righteous man and walked with God. I believe it is important to understand that vision from God comes to righteous, blameless men and women that walk with Him. I believe it is critical that we, as leaders in the local church and as church planners, are righteous and blameless among the people of our time.

I start each day in my office walking with God. Sometimes I just sit in my office, reading His Word. Other days I spend time talking to Him. On other mornings, I literally walk with Him around the office praying for my projects and for the other architects that are part of our team. I believe that both vision and spiritual blessing comes from God. I also believe that such vision and blessing is bestowed upon those that walk with God.

NOAH BUILT IT EXACTLY ACCORDING TO PLAN. IT WAS THE PLAN FROM THE LORD AND IT FLOATED.

It is also an important truth that the plans came specifically from the Lord. The Lord spoke to Noah and told him to make an ark of cypress wood. He was to make individual rooms, coat it with pitch inside and out. The Lord gave him the length, width and height and told him that he was to finish it within 18 in. of the very top. He was to build it three floors deep and he was to build it according to the plan.

I firmly believe that if Noah had not followed the specific plans of God including the minor, seemingly insignificant plan such as finishing the ark to within 18 in. of the top, all of mankind could have been wiped out by the forty days of rain.

Noah was not only a righteous man, but he was a man of details. God gave him the plan, the dimensions and the finishing materials. Noah built it exactly according to plan. It was the plan from the Lord and it floated. Today we are witnesses of that as we all are descendants of Noah and his family.

Noah walked with God, God gave him the plans and Noah responded by following God's plans to the minute detail. The result of walking with the Lord and following His plans was salvation to the entire household of

Noah. If we walk with the Lord, as Noah walked with the Lord, I believe we can live with the spirit of expectancy concerning these things of God. I believe we can expect God to give us vision, plans and wisdom specifically as He did for Noah.

I also believe that the result of us following such plans will be significant ministry within the local church, as salvation will come to the households of many. Certainly Noah and the building of the ark is a fine example that we can follow in our own building projects.

The Tabernacle of Moses...

Moses lived a rich life and set his heart upon following the Lord as well. Moses spent approximately 40 years living as a king with the Pharaoh's family of Egypt. He then spent the second 40 years of his existence as a shepherd. The first third of his life he spent living as a somebody (in the eyes of man). The second third of his life he spent living as a lowly shepherd (or as a nobody) in the eyes of man.

But then the word of God came to Moses and he spent the last 40 years living as a servant of God with the understanding that God is indeed everything. It was during his last 40 years, as he led the people through the wilderness venture of Sinai, that the word of the Lord came to Moses as follows:

"Tell the Israelites to bring me an offering. You are to receive the offering for me from each man whose heart prompts him to give. These are the offerings you are to receive from them: gold, silver, and bronze; blue, purple, and scarlet yarn and fine linen; goat hair; ram skins dyed red and hides of seacow; acacia wood; olive oil for the light; spices for the anointing oil and for the fragrant incense; and onyx stones and other gems to be mounted on the ephod and breast piece. Then have them make a sanctuary for me and I will dwell among them. Make this tabernacle and all of its furnishings exactly like the pattern I will show you."
— Exodus 25:2-9

It is interesting that Moses, similar to Noah, had no experience specifically building tabernacles for a holy God. It is true that he had built structures and had been an overseer in the land of the Pharaoh. However, the entire process of building a sanctuary for a holy God to dwell amongst his people was new with Moses.

It is also interesting that, similar to Noah, the vision came from the Lord. God gave him the specific plans. Earlier in this chapter, I recorded the scripture from I Chronicles 17:2 that states "Carry out the plan and every detail, for it is the will of the Lord." This is reflected again in the scripture whereby God gives very detailed building instructions to Moses.

He states in verse 9, "Make this tabernacle and all its furnishings exactly like the pattern I will show you." You might wish to read the account for yourself. The pattern that He showed him is clearly stated in Exodus 25, Exodus 26 and Exodus 27. Three complete chapters are dedicated in the Word of God to this "exact pattern" which the Lord gave Moses.

God described the tabernacle. God also described and gave details of the lamp stand, the cups, the wick trimmers and trays and the seven lamps. He then communicated His intent for the curtains, the fifty loops of the curtains, the bronze clasps to hold them together and the frames of the tent. He completed His master plan by stating the design details of the crossbars, the horizontal bars, the altar, the entrance, the ark of the testimony, the carrying poles and the courtyard. It is easy to see that God had specific instructions and details for Moses.

It is also important to notice that the entire provision for this great undertaking was to be provided by the Lord but through the people. The scripture stated above in Exodus 25, verse 2, states that the Lord instructed Moses to "tell the Israelites to bring me an offering." The Lord then told Moses the specifics of the offerings. It is apparent to me that the Lord not only spoke to Moses regarding the instructions of the provision but also spoke to the hearts of the people. Ultimately, Moses went to the people and asked them to stop giving as they had enough. When the Lord does the providing, the provisions are always enough for the work. There was plenty of provision. Moses was able to carry out in exact detail everything that the Lord had instructed him to do.

The result of Noah following God's commandments was the salvation of the people. Moses, too, followed all of God's directives for the tabernacle. The result of his obedience was the presence of an almighty God. I firmly believe that if Moses had changed the plan or changed the details, God most likely would have not shown up to inhabit the tabernacle. He told Moses to build this tabernacle "exactly" according to pattern. Moses walked in obedience and the result of that obedience was God's glory inhabiting the place.

There is another interesting story that is weaved within this tabernacle building process that I wish to note. It is the story of two of my favorite characters in the Old Testament. You may have never heard of the characters of Bezalel and Oholiab.

Consider the following scriptures:

"Then Moses said of the Israelites, 'See, the Lord has chosen Bezalel, son of Uri, the son of Uhur, of the tribe of Judah and He has filled him with the spirit of God, with skill, ability and knowledge and all kinds of crafts to make artistic designs for working gold, silver, and bronze, to cut and set stones, to work in wood and to engage in all kinds of artistic craftsmanship. And He has given both him and Oholiab, son of Ahisamach, the tribe of Dan, the ability to teach others.

He has filled them with skill to do all kinds of work as craftsman, designers, embroiderers in blue, purple and scarlet yarn and fine linen, and weavers-all of them master craftsmen and designers. So Bezalel and Oholiab and every skilled person to whom the Lord has given skill and ability to know how to carry out all the work of constructing the sanctuary are to do the work just as the Lord commanded.' Then Moses summoned Bezalel and Oholiab and every skilled person to whom the Lord had given ability and who was willing to come and do the work."
— Exodus 35:30-36:2

God gave Moses the vision. As this applies to current-day construction of facilities to house the local church, I believe God gives the pastor spiritual vision. The pastor communicates the vision to his leadership, and the leadership communicates this vision of the church's particular ministry to the architect. The architect is to understand and grasp the vision that God has given to the pastoral staff.

However, we as architects relate more specifically to Bezalel and Oholiab of the scriptures above. They were the skilled designers and craftspeople. They were the master designers as Moses stated in Exodus 35, verse 35. It is interesting that the Lord states in Exodus 35:31 that "he has filled him, Bezalel" with the skilled ability and knowledge and all kinds of crafts to make artistic designs. The application of this truth is quite apparent to us as architects. It is God that fills our personal tabernacles with His Spirit and it is He that gives us the skill, ability and knowledge to make such artistic designs.

Though it was Bezalel that had the ability to design, it was Oholiab that God had given the skill and ability to teach others. Bezalel and Oholiab form an interesting architectural team for the carrying out of the tabernacle. The vision came from God to Moses. The Spirit of God filled Bezalel in order that he would have the skill, ability and knowledge to make such artistic designs.

However, God knew that this was a tremendous undertaking and Bezalel could not handle it alone. Therefore, God gave Oholiab the specific gifting of the "ability to teach others." Together they formed a wonderfully blessed spirit-filled architectural office. This gave them the opportunity to duplicate their efforts in the design profession and to ultimately assist Moses in the carrying out of God's plans for the tabernacle. This wonderfully conceived and designed tabernacle ultimately housed the Spirit of God for the journey of the people of Israel through Sinai.

The Temple of Solomon
Solomon was the son of King David and ultimately took over the throne of David when David died. As you might remember, David brought the Ark of the Covenant back into Jerusalem and danced in front of the processional. However, the Ark of the Covenant never had a permanent home through David's reign. It was Solomon who built the great temple in Jerusalem in order to house the Ark of the Covenant there.

When David realized that he had built for himself a great palace of cedar, he then realized that it was only proper that he build one for God as well. The Ark of the Covenant had been housed in a tent ever since Moses built the tabernacle. Therefore David's son would set the plans in motion to build a house or a temple for the Ark of the Lord.

The word of God in Chronicles expresses the clear fact that David planned the entire temple and even accumulated the tremendous wealth and gifts needed for the actual building. But it was Solomon, his son, who actually built the temple. Consider the following scriptures:

"'And you, my son Solomon, acknowledge the God of your father, and serve Him with wholehearted devotion and with a willing mind, for the Lord searches every heart and understands every motive behind the thoughts. If you seek Him, He will be found by you; but if you forsake Him He will reject you forever. Consider now, for the Lord has chosen you to build a temple as a sanctuary. Be strong and do the work.'

Then David gave his son Solomon the plans for the portico of the temple, its buildings, its storerooms, its upper parts, its inner rooms and the place of atonement. He gave him the plans of all that the spirit had put in his mind for the courts of the temple of the Lord and all the surrounding rooms, for the treasuries of the temple of God and for the treasuries for the dedicated things."
— I Chronicles 28:9-12

Similar to our two examples above, the ark of Noah and the tabernacle of Moses, Solomon had no experience in temple building. In fact, David was really not an architect. When we think of David, we often see him as the young shepherd boy or we picture him as the brave young man that took on Goliath. We also picture him as the warrior that he was. A great deal of David's heart is communicated to us through the Psalms, which he wrote. We see David as an incredible king that loved God with all of his heart. He was the King that loved music and poetry.

Many of the Psalms were actually written by David himself and reflect the times and various crises of his life. However, we have never really viewed King David as an architect running an architectural company and designing the temple as he ran the kingdom. However, the scriptures above are very clear.

In this I Chronicles chapter 8 portion of scripture, King David is quite old and about to die. He is sitting with his son, King Solomon, who has been chosen to actually build the temple as a sanctuary for God. He encourages his son to be strong and do the work. It is very clear in verse 11 that King David gave his son Solomon the plans for the entire temple.

> Where does vision come from?
> Vision is direct Spirit revelation from God.
> Where do plans come from?
> The scripture tells us that plans also come from the Lord.

Verse 12 of chapter 28 in I Chronicles states, "He gave him (Solomon) the plans of all that the Spirit had put in his mind for the courts in the temple of the Lord...." It is obvious from the scripture that King David knew where the plans for the temple came from. The specific plans of the temple, the surrounding rooms, as well as the financing of the temple, came from the Spirit of God. All David had to do was to record the plans and pass them along to his son Solomon. Solomon would ultimately build the great temple for the Lord.

WE HAVE NEVER REALLY VIEWED KING DAVID AS AN ARCHITECT RUNNING AN ARCHITECTURAL COMPANY AND DESIGNING THE TEMPLE AS HE RAN THE KINGDOM.

The provision also was from the Lord. The same verse states that he also gave Solomon what the Spirit had communicated to him regarding "the treasuries of the temple of God and for the treasuries for the dedicated things." The Lord does not give us direction or a mission without giving us the provisions for that mission. God provides us with what we need for us to do his work. The provisions and the necessary items for the building of

the temple were planned by the Lord, communicated by His spirit to David and passed along to Solomon.

God utilized King David in a tremendous way and history records such. However, we do hear very little of King David's architectural department that must have "penned" down all that the Holy Spirit had communicated to the King. The result of King David following the Lord's leading resulted in his son having plans to build the temple for the next generation. Once the temple was built, the result was the same.

God showed up and His glory filled the temple.

What more could a local church request from God at the conclusion of a building project? I can think of no greater blessing than for God to show up and to greet us with His presence. Now I know that we are no longer building sanctuaries to house the Spirit of the Lord. However, the parallel is quite apparent.

If we follow the Lord's leading in all that He would have us do, He will fulfill His vision for the local church. He will provide provision for the local church and ultimately give us the physical facilities that we need in order to provide the ministry that He wishes for us to provide.

The Lord's glory will shine upon us.

 Lives will be changed...

...and the community will be a different place because of it.

PERSONAL OBSERVATIONS

I have sensed the leading of the Lord on many projects over the last 25 years in my office. I have sensed His blessings on the architectural design of many different particular facilities. Several years back, we received a phone call from a local pastor who desired to build a three million-dollar Christian elementary school facility for the children of the community. He had received direct revelation from the Lord concerning this. Acreage was purchased and we were ultimately commissioned for the design of the project.

I can remember pausing before the beginning of the preliminary drawings and asking God to bless us in our endeavors that we might understand the will of the Lord concerning the ultimate design of the elementary school.

As I began to layout the specific design for the Christian school, the concept struck me regarding a prayer garden that would be a central area around which all of the classrooms would radiate. Not only would the Word of God be central to the lives of the school, but the prayer garden that would be utilized for devotionals to teach the children the Word of God would be central (physically) within the plans of the entire facility. Classrooms would radiate around the prayer garden, and the design ultimately took the shape of a large octagon.

We continued to work on the design as we continued to pray. Our prayer, as architects on the project, was not some mystical statement or spiritual whim to God. It was a very simple and humble prayer that we might be utilized as His servants, no different than King David when he recorded the plans that the Holy Spirit had given him in his mind for the temple.

I will never forget the day that we finished the actual plans. The preliminary floor plan was complete and the preliminary building elevation was finished, and we met with that particular pastor on a sunny Monday afternoon. I opened the roll of drawings slowly and began to walk him through the facility. I spoke to him regarding the prayer garden concept, and I showed him how the individual classrooms radiated out around the central prayer garden symbolizing how the Word of God would be central to the life of the children within their own Christian school.

The pastor sat in silence for what seemed like hours looking at the floor plan. He looked at the building elevations and then looked back at the floor plan. After what seemed like an eternity of space and time, the pastor looked up to me with moistened eyes. I will never forget the question that he asked that day...

"Let me ask you something Michael, how much of this is the product of your mental capability of putting a project together and how much of this is a result of the Spirit of God?"

It was amazing to me that he had asked such a question. He was basically asking, "Did we come up with the design ourselves or was this product a result of inspiration?"

I sat in silence for awhile, not knowing exactly how to address the question or answer the inquiry. How does one separate mind and spirit? We had prayed for the leading of the Lord, and we had felt God's anointing upon the project. Nevertheless, I was not able to say for certain how much of our final design had to do with spirit revelation as compared to standard architectural design work. I simply expressed it to him in that way. And then I asked him a question...

"Why do you ask?"

"I really wanted to know because I would have never been able to draw this on paper, but you need to know this is exactly what the Lord would have us to build. It is exactly what I had in my mind's eye. I believe that this came from the Father, and I believe this is what God would have us to build."

I was awestruck.

I won't forget leaving that meeting and driving back to the office thanking the Lord for the fact that he can anoint us as architectural designers.

WE STRIVE ON EVERY PROJECT TO DESIGN IN ACCORDANCE WITH THE WILL OF THE LORD, AS GOD MOVES UPON OUR HEARTS DURING THE DESIGN PROCESS.

I could really say that I had given that Pastor the plans of all that I felt the Spirit had put in our mind. Now I am not about to say that every project is completed in exactly the same way as that Christian School.

However, we strive on every project to design in accordance with the will of the Lord, as God moves upon our hearts during the design process. The design process of the local church is a spiritual matter. It should not be taken lightly. The selection of your church architect should not be taken lightly as well.

On that same school, I experienced an event that blessed my entire office. The church building the elementary school decided that they would pray on a regular basis for the men that were working on the building. They would continue to pray for the subcontractors, the superintendent, as well as the material suppliers. I had grown quite fond of a particular gentleman by the name of Jim. He was an excellent superintendent and worked very hard to make certain that the elementary school would be built in accordance with our construction drawings. However, he was not a Christian. He continued to build the building and put his imprint of care and concern upon all the details of the particular project.

However, I will never forget the day that I drove up to the job site, parked my car and walked into the building. Jim looked at me sheepishly and said, "Guess what?" I responded thinking that perhaps we had a problem on the job site or a challenge that needed to be solved. Jim quickly stated to me that he was a different man. In the process of building the building, Jim had met a young lady and attended church with her. That Sunday, he had gone forward at the church and given his life to the Lord and was a new creature.

Now I had a born-again Christian as a superintendent running the project job. Not only did he work hard on a daily basis, but he now felt that the Lord's hand was upon him specifically to guide the subcontractors and material suppliers on the particular job. In fact, his professional direction as well as his spiritual walk has resulted in a tremendous amount of character being reflected within his work. This has caused the client to request him specifically on a two million-dollar gymnasium, a five million-dollar church, as well as a six million-dollar middle school.

God does work in mysterious ways. Now it is interesting to note that the building did go up with brick and mortar. However, the process was much more than brick and mortar. The process was a spiritual one. We believe that the plan of the actual facility was communicated through God's Spirit to our spirit during the preliminary design process. God assisted us in the building of the structure and ultimately saved the superintendent in the process.

Never forget that the building process for the local church is certainly a spiritual event. I have seen many miracles throughout my 25 years of serving the local church.

I have seen church buildings that needed to be sold...sell at the appropriate time.

I have witnessed churches that needed land, find land...at the appropriate time.

THE BUILDING PROCESS FOR THE LOCAL CHURCH IS CERTAINLY A SPIRITUAL EVENT.

I have seen building committees and church boards pray together and seek God together. I have seen those boards ultimately be unified so that the Lord could work within their church building process. I often stress the importance of unity amongst a church building committee or church board. It is difficult for a building committee or a board to not be in unison about a particular project and take the project drawings to the church body as a whole. In many cases such as that, I have witnessed the church body model their leadership and ultimately split on the vote as well. However, I have often seen leadership boards pray for unity amongst the board in regard to design decisions that have to be made throughout the design process. In every case, spiritual unity on the board resulted in a true spiritual unity amongst the people.

The journey truly is a spiritual one.

YOUR SPIRITUAL JOURNEY

Throughout the master planning, the preliminary drawings, the construction drawings and ultimately the construction of your project, there will be numerous decisions and challenges that you will face regarding the physical "brick and mortar." You will be faced with critical decisions regarding:

> The type of structure
> The type of heating and cooling units
> Chandeliers or recessed lights, or both
> Concrete block or steel frame construction
> Flat roof or steep roof
> Metal roof or shingled roof
> Brick exterior or stucco exterior
> Color of the carpet
> Color of the pews

I could go on and on as you will also be faced with many challenges regarding the local municipalities. You may face meetings with the planning department, meetings with the planning commission, meetings with the city council, meetings with historical architectural review boards, meetings with city or county architectural design committees. It will be very easy for the architect and the building committee as a whole to focus on the challenges of the "brick and mortar" issues. However, it is also very critical to continually remind yourself of the spiritual journey that you are undertaking.

SPIRITUAL WARFARE IS REAL AND IT CAN AFFECT THE PLANNING AND BUILDING OF THE LOCAL CHURCH.

It is a spiritual journey. You are building for the glory of God. You are building to further God's kingdom here on earth.

You will face difficulties. In fact, I have seen churches enter into the building process only to find themselves in a spiritual war. Spiritual warfare is real and it can affect the planning and building of the local church.

The devil certainly doesn't want your ministry to continue to grow and your influence for God to be enlarged in your community. He will do everything he can to resist you.

It is important that the committee, the pastor and the architect remain "prayed up" throughout the process. Always remind yourself that you are on a spiritual journey.

The vision comes from God.
The provision comes from God.
In fact, all 'good and perfect gifts' come from above.

It is important to remain in prayerful unity throughout the process. As I pointed out above, timing is important. Pray for God's revelation of His timetable.

You must remain a team that believes. If God spoke this vision into your heart, embark on this spiritual journey with all the vision, prayer, unity and faith that the Holy Spirit has put inside you. Always remember that though it appears we are building the building, every good and perfect gift really comes from above.

David states it most plainly in Psalms 127:1.

"Unless the Lord builds the house, its builders labor in vain."

Let us not labor in vain. Let's remember that the Lord builds the house. We are making the plans, but we are counting on God to direct us. We are to be strong and courageous and not be afraid and discouraged for God is with us.

He will not fail us and He will not forsake us until our work is finished.

Embark upon the spiritual journey and enjoy it. For when the journey is complete, the result will be many salvations in the Kingdom of God.

Let's take this journey together.■

PHASES OF THE BUILDING DELIVERY PROCESS 4
Steps from Inception to Dedication

There are six major phases of a typical church building program. They are as follows:

1 > Owner Survey phase
2 > Pre-Planning phase
3 > Preliminary Master Planing Design phase
4 > Construction Drawing phase
5 > Construction phase
6 > Post Construction phase

In this chapter, I will analyze the different phases of the building delivery process. We will explore the areas of responsibility of both the architect as well as the church. Each phase of the process is an equally important one that needs to be understood by the local church.

Though the church, as the client, needs to have an understanding of these phases, it is ultimately the church architect that is responsible in educating the client regarding these phases and tasks per phase.

Let's now look briefly at each phase of this process. Each phase will be discussed and explained. Tasks relating to each phase will then be identified and listed for your review.

OWNER SURVEY PHASE

This is the phase whereby the owner surveys their existing situation and determines that they need either a new building, a renovation of an existing building or an additional space to accommodate a new or growing ministry. This owner survey phase may be a very specific organized study by a building committee or architect, or it may be as loose as a general feeling of a pastor, co-pastor or staff member on board.

Occasionally, when a new church is beginning to build for the first time, the owner survey phase may include a study of potential neighborhoods in which to relocate. It may also include investigation into areas where land or existing buildings (to renovate) are available throughout their city. This phase, for a new church plant, may even include specific studies of the demographics of a particular area.

For an existing church that has an existing building, it may be that they have outgrown their worship facility or their Christian Education facility. On some occasions, ministries will change or expand giving rise to the need for additional specific physical facilities that are not yet present.

Often, the architect is contacted after the owner has determined their need. However, there are occasions when the architect is contacted to assist in this owner survey phase. The owner may identify the need and request the assistance of the professional architect to help them in this early phase of expansion. At this time, the architect can assist the owner in evaluating their spatial needs. The architect may even head-up and direct the surveying efforts of their existing building.

THE OWNER SURVEY PHASE TASKS

A > Organize the church's efforts:

1 > Often, the first step of the church during the survey phase is the organization of a long-range planning or building committee to assist the pastor in the evaluation of the needs.

2 > The church will select a church architect with suitable experience in church design to assist in this early process.

B > The committee will begin the investigation and research of the existing situation (It is recommended that an architect assist in this phase):

1 > The first step of the committee is the evaluation and study of all initial space requirements and the amount of property needed by the church.

2 > The church may want to research the demographics of the community in determining growth potential and programs needed.

3 > Investigate space requirements for all the church's programs, including a study and listing of the present church programs and use of the present building.

4 > Investigate future space needs required by the growing programs within the church. The committee should attempt to project growth in 5 years, 10 years and 20 years.

5 > Study the church's financial condition including the maximum amount of funds, which can be safely borrowed.

During this survey phase, a church (often with the assistance of their church architect) seeks out, secures and analyzes the church community. They may also investigate and analyze church property and perhaps evaluate the physical condition of any existing facilities. From this survey information, programs of requirements are proposed and the type and amount of space is realistically determined. This next phase is the pre-planning phase.

PRE-PLANNING PHASE

This is the phase of a building program that is most often left out of the overall process. It is not unusual for an owner to survey their ministry needs and to contact an architect to immediately begin design on a new building. However, the pre-planning phase is a very specific and unique phase that is very important if a church is going to fully identify their various challenges and evaluate them.

During this phase, the church architect will assist the church leadership in the overall evaluation of their challenges. The architect will explore the church leadership's vision and mission statement. Ultimately, the architect will prepare the following documents for the use of the church in their final design and planning:

> Project Goals and Objectives
> Vision Statement
> Spatial Analysis of Need
> Opinion of Construction Cost

Let us look at these processes and define the documents individually.

PROJECT GOALS AND OBJECTIVES

The pre-planning phase consists of the architect assisting the church in the establishment of goals and objectives. The process is typically one where the architect asks questions of the church in order to assist them in crystallizing the overall goals and objectives of their building project. In many cases, specific building components are not discussed at this phase, but the overall needs and goals are identified.

It is the responsibility of the architect to assist the owner in this difficult stage by drawing out from the committee the foundational needs and goals of their project. Spiritual needs are often addressed. Physical spatial needs are addressed as well. It is not uncommon to discuss various ideas such as image, architectural symbolism and the liturgical symbols that should be utilized within the final design. At the completion of this research, a final "Goals and Objectives" document is prepared for the final approval of the building committee.

VISION STATEMENT

It is during this phase that the overall vision of the church and its ministry is discussed and established, if it is not already formulated. The architect's ultimate goal during the preliminary design phase (the next phase) is to explore the possible design solutions as they relate to the pastor's vision. Therefore, it is critical to establish and document the church's vision in order to keep the designer and church building committee accountable to the pastor's vision.

Often, the pastor has already established the vision of the ministry. Occasionally, I find that the vision is an old vision written by a pastor who has long left the fellowship. Or it may be that the vision has not already been crystallized and written down for the ministry leadership team to pray about and internalize. In this case, it is important for the architect to gently lead the church team in the establishment of such a vision statement.

I believe that the vision for the 'local church' comes from God. That vision flows from God to the Senior Pastor to his staff and leadership and then ultimately to the architect. It is our purpose to align our final design with the Pastor's vision. Once the vision is fully understood and developed, it is then verbally articulated by the architect within the "Vision Statement" document.

SPATIAL ANALYSIS OF NEED

Another important component of the pre-planning phase is the square foot "Spatial Analysis of Need" which addresses the actual physical components required by the church in order to effectively achieve their overall objectives. Again, the building itself is not yet the issue, but the need of the church is the issue being studied. The actual spatial needs and requirements are now being identified.

The architect can fully assist the church by not only helping to establish the critical needs of their ministry, but he can also assist the church in establishing specific square footages required for the individual spaces. These numbers, representing sizes of spaces, are often based upon an estimated occupant count. The result of this pre-planning is a spatial square foot analysis plan that begins to establish the parameters of the project in square feet. This reflects the ministry need identified in the owner survey phase.

OPINION OF CONSTRUCTION COST

The final step in the pre-planning phase is to apply specific budget numbers to the square foot analysis to establish overall preliminary budgets of proposed solutions to the ministry space needs. This is a very important document in that it establishes an initial cost for those needs addressed in the spatial analysis.

The entire concept of biblical financial considerations is fully covered in Chapter 11, "Financial Considerations." Therefore, I will not attempt to fully address this important concept at this time.

However, the biblical concept of 'counting the cost' is of the utmost importance at this stage. It is critical to account for the costing of the project to determine if the preliminary costs which reflect the church's goals, objectives and spatial needs are indeed in line with their anticipated budget. Often, the preliminary cost considerations far exceed the anticipated available funds for the church. When this occurs, it is easy to review the project goals and objectives and determine what areas need to be reduced in order to align the cost with budget. Once the final costs are approved, the budget is documented in an "Opinion of Construction Cost" for the design phase.

PRE-PLANNING PHASE TASKS
A > Development of the Program

1 > The church architect will analyze and evaluate all survey and research materials established within the owner survey phase.

2 > The architect will prepare a well-documented "Goals and Objectives" statement. This should include all of the goals of the project. This proposal should include an overall projection of programs needed currently and in the future.

3 > The architect will then document the church vision in a "Vision Statement" document for future reference in the design phase.

4 > The functional needs of the expansion are then evaluated in terms of square ft. of space actually needed. This will result in a "Square Foot Spatial Analysis of Need" which should be prepared and documented by the architect.

B > Financial Proposal

1 > During this phase of the project, the team may want to identify the sources of financing for the proposed building project.

2 > A well-qualified church architect can be instrumental in providing the "Opinion of Construction Cost" which will guide the church in determining the ultimate cost of their proposed venture.

3 > The final plans for the capital campaign are often now started. However, they are not completed until the architect has completed the following phase, which is the master planning design phase.

C > Reporting Recommendations to the Church Board or Body

1 > When the written program proposal including the above documents has been completed, a report can then be made to the entire church board, if necessary.

2 > The report (if needed) should include all of the recommendations concerning programs needed, estimates of the amount of property required and its cost and the amount of building space to be constructed. The three documents above can best be utilized to communicate this to the church as a whole.

PRELIMINARY MASTER PLANNING DESIGN PHASE

During the preliminary master planning design phase, the architect establishes the preliminary plans for the owner to review. These might include master phasing plans, preliminary site plans, preliminary floor plans and layout plans, as well as building elevations. Architects often refer to these preliminary plans as 'schematic plans.' It is during this phase that the architect will quite often prepare some type of perspective rendering addressing the overall aesthetics of the project.

The designed floor plans and other drawings should be in harmony with the church's programs, needs and objectives. It is during this time that the "Goals and Objectives," the "Opinion of Construction Cost," the "Vision Statement" and "Square Foot Spatial Analysis" should be revisited to insure a proper 'fitness' between the design and these initial parameters of the project. Both the church architect and the church building committee should be accountable to these initial parameters and goals which have been defined and approved in order to guide the team through the design process.

It is during this phase that the architect provides computer generated 3-D architectural renderings and computer animations to better communicate the design solution to the church. We call this "Vision Casting." In fact, we often assist the pastor in planning a special "Vision Casting" service where the 3-D renderings and final animations are presented to the church.

During this phase the architect may also assist the owner in identifying any other phases of the work. It is not unusual for a church to have ministry needs whose costs well exceed their financial capability. Therefore, a complete master plan, which identifies the various phases of construction, is very important. Master plans illustrating many different phases may be proposed at this time.

Fund-raising programs are then set in motion. The church will begin to evaluate their budget and building cost requirements. The church is then in a position to proceed with the architect on working drawing documents for the construction of the project during the following phase.

PRELIMINARY MASTER PLANNING DESIGN PHASE TASKS
A > Development of Master Site Plans

1> The architect should develop a master plan site layout of the property before any building is planned. This assures proper location of the current building and the location of all future buildings.

B > Development of Schematic Preliminary Drawings

1> These drawings are primarily for the purpose of showing, in graphic floor plan form, program space to meet the needs of the church. From them, rough cost estimates can be calculated. They may or may not be the actual shape and arrangement of the final design.

C > Development of Defined Schematic Plans

1> Schematic plans are the drawings prepared for the purpose of showing the architect's proposed building arrangement, its location on the property and the elevations of the building, as well as the overall aesthetic design concept of the project.

D > Development of 3-D computer virtual reality renderings and computer animations

E > Report Recommendations to the Church

1 > When the architect's schematics completed and reviewed by the responsible committees and cost proposals are projected for the building and furnishings, a report should be made to the church.

2 > Copies of the drawings should be presented by the church architect to the church body as a whole. Ample opportunity should be given to the church members to ask the architect questions or make suggestions.

F > Church Action

1 > Approval of the final presentation drawings by the church or its governmental body.

G > Financial Proposal and Capital Campaign

1 > During this phase of the project, the sources of financing for the proposed building project are investigated and tentative plans are made for raising and/or borrowing funds.

2 > A well-qualified church architect can be instrumental in providing the documents needed to start the campaign.

CONSTRUCTION DRAWING PHASE

Once the master-planning documents have been completed and budgets have been established, the architect enters into the construction document phase. It is during this phase whereby the architect actually prepares and furnishes the final construction documents utilized by the contractor for actual construction of the project.

The architect's role throughout this phase is similar to that of a conductor. He brings a variety of individuals to the team in order to successfully put together a complete set of construction drawings. The following consultants are utilized during most projects during the construction drawing phase:

> Plumbing engineering consultants
> Mechanical/Heating/Cooling engineering consultants
> Electrical engineering consultants
> Special lighting consultants

> Interior Design consultants
> Structural engineering consultants
> Civil/Site engineering consultants

The conclusion of this phase provides the church with complete construction drawings, as well as book specifications suitable for applying for final building permits from their local building authority. It also provides suitable documentation whereby contractors can provide competitive bids for the project.

CONSTRUCTION DRAWING PHASE TASKS
A > Project Design Development

1 > With the schematics completed and approved by the church, the architect can be instructed to go ahead with developing the project design. This includes the selection of materials, building methodologies and systems.

B > Project Design Development Reviews and Approvals

1 > When the architect has completed the various design development decisions, the appropriate committee should review them. With approval of the design development and updated cost estimates, the committee is ready to release the architect to complete the final architectural construction drawings. These are often referred to as working drawings.

C > Construction Drawings and Specifications

1 > Having completed the master site design, interior floor plan and exterior design, the architect is now ready to develop the construction working drawings and book specifications for the construction of the project.

2 > These are periodically reviewed by the church building committee.

CONSTRUCTION PHASE

It is during this phase that the owner, with the assistance of the architect, selects a contractor for construction. Prices are gathered and occasionally the project may be bid to several contractors. See Chapter 6 for a full explanation of 'Partnering.' Once the final construction cost and bids have been prepared by the approved contractor and accepted by the church, the contractor begins construction.

The architect, owner and contractor will often meet periodically to review the course of construction. The architect will make periodic visits to the site to assure the client that the construction is in accordance with the contract documents that were prepared by the architect and approved by the church. This phase ends with a successful completion of the building phase by the contractor, approvals of the building by the architect and the ultimate use of the building by the owner.

CONSTRUCTION PHASE TASKS
A > Recommend the Contractor

B > Bids Let and Received

C > Church Action

1 > When the church receives the recommendation from the committee, it should take official action on accepting the contract and the contractor.

D > Get Furnishings Bid

1 > Pews
2 > Sound System
3 > Furnishings, Fixtures and Equipment

E > Secure the Construction and Furnishings Loan

1 > With the construction and furnishings contracts signed, a church now knows the exact amount of financing it will need.

2 > At this time, the committee completes transactions for the loan with the lending agency selected previously by the church.

F > Project Construction

G > Inspections of Work

1 > At specified intervals during the construction period, the architect will make inspections of the construction.

H > Furnish the Building

1 > The furnishings for the building should be installed at the time the building is completed.

I > Final Inspection

1 > The architect provides the final inspection of the built facility.

2 > The architect provides a "Punch List" to the contractor and client. This is a complete listing of the items that the contractor needs to complete in order to receive from the architect a final certificate of completion.

POST CONSTRUCTION EVALUATION PHASE

This phase seems to be the most neglected phase of all the phases of the building program. It is important that the architect follow up with the church after the construction has been completed and the church has occupied their new facility. This is for the purpose of reviewing warranties, as well as reviewing the overall performance of the building. At this time, the architect can review the performance of the individual components and subsystems of the building. These may include:

> Heating systems
> Cooling systems
> Elevator and associated equipment
> Roofing integrity
> Parking lot
> Fixtures and furnishings

In the event that there are any problems that need to be solved, the architect can contact the contractor within the one-year warranty period and make certain that all work is taken care of in a timely fashion.

POST CONSTRUCTION EVALUATION PHASE TASKS
A > Beyond the Construction Phase

1 > There are two categories of the work to be continued beyond the construction phase. One of these is maintenance and the other is repaying the construction and furnishings loan.

a > Maintenance — The continuing maintenance of the church building (including the keys) should be turned over to the regular church property and space committee.

b > Financing — The regular church finance committee then assumes the responsibility of administering the financial program until its completion.

PARTNERING PROCESS
(Optional — See Chapter 6 for a full explanation)
Though many projects during the 70's and 80's were built using the standard design-bid-build process, the process of partnering has gradually grown in its popularity for various reasons. Though the entire process of partnering will be discussed in another chapter, the following is a brief discussion of the process:

A > Partnering

1 > The significant difference between partnering and other construction methods is in the increased degree of input and responsibility by a contractor during early design. The guaranteed maximum price (GMP) can usually be given quite early in the process.

2 > Under partnering, the GMP is typically provided at the 10% - 15% design completion level. This assures that the owner will get the building he wants, as defined by an early agreed upon cost.

B > Price Testing

1 > Partnering provides price testing of multiple concepts before design drawing changes become very costly.

2 > This allows the owner a greater deal of design control as critical decisions concerning various concepts can be based upon factual cost information and not speculative estimates.

3 > This unique team effort, involving the owner, most often reduces construction costs on a project.

4 > Partnering provides custom tailored, cost effective solutions to the owner's needs and problems with concepts to meet the owner's goals.

C > Team Effort

1 > Partnering provides the framework allowing the efforts of many individuals to be utilized simultaneously.

2 > As a percentage of the total project schedule, more time can be saved during the pre-construction phase than during the actual construction phase.

3 > Under partnering, the time to prepare construction documents is less. The plan approval process, with various municipal agencies, can be managed by the contractor simultaneously with the construction document process.

D > Value Engineering

1 > A valuable tool is "Value Engineering." Throughout the planning and design phase, a thorough evaluation can be carried out to show the effect of alternatives on cost, time and quality. What works best on one project may not serve the next one.

2 > The design schedule cost and quality of each project is a complicated process uniquely dictated by the owner's objective, site characteristics and regulatory constraints.

3 > Value engineering of the best options can be performed by the partnering team.

E > Fast Tracking

1 > Partnering provides the possibility of fast tracked construction scheduling. With the fast track method, construction is started before the entire design is complete.

2 > This can allow for the commencement of site work, the building of the foundation and the purchase of long lead items before the contract documents are even finished. This is one of the most valuable contributions of the team effort.

SUMMARY

It is important to note that all six phases of this process are critical to the overall success of any church building program. It would be difficult to begin this process without the initial owner survey phase whereby the owner begins to both recognize his ministry needs and then document such needs.

Without the proper pre-planning, many goals and objectives may be left out of the design process. The statement of vision and the initial budgeting initiatives are vital for an overall successful campaign. It is during this phase that God can so richly and divinely communicate His vision and purpose for the church campaign.

The preliminary master plan design phase provides the owner with the first initial visual representation of the project solution. The construction drawings are important as they communicate the overall structural and architectural components to the contractor. And without the ultimate construction phase, no building is built and no vision is realized.

And last, the post construction phase allows for communication between the entire team in order to assure that all designed components of the project are indeed operating in their designed and desired purpose.

If there is any major deviation of this process or elimination of these phases, the final product, and perhaps the final ministry, of the church may suffer. Only a skilled, experienced church architect should be engaged to assist you on this journey. Each of these phases are uniquely and especially designed to guide you on this God-directed pilgrimage.

Let's walk through these phases together...

> Owner Survey phase
> Pre-Planning phase
> Preliminary Master Planing Design phase
> Construction Drawing phase
> Construction phase
> Post Construction phase

Though your architect should be thoroughly trained in all of these areas, never forget that it is God that guides you.

I know He will.

We have experienced it and you can too!■

EXPANDABILITY AND ADAPTABILITY 5
Growth of Your Physical Facilities

EXPANSION NEEDS OF MINISTRY

Churches and worship spaces are built to accommodate people. When the local church is serving its purpose of evangelizing their community, the number of people within that church will naturally grow. The Gospel, rightly divided and pronounced, always perpetuates growth. This is, and should be, a natural component of the Christian community. As the number of worshippers grow in any particular congregation, the physical facilities which were designed and built yesterday are not suitable to meet the needs of today.

The adaptability prerequisite and the growth requirement of the physical facilities of the local church is perhaps more demanding on the professional architect than any other type of commercial design project. Offices seldom have the need to expand in the same way that worship facilities do. Shopping centers and restaurants seldom have the distinct necessity of expanding their physical facilities like a church. However, the local church that is growing within their community will always be faced with the problem of matching their physical facilities to their ministry needs at hand.

There are two major approaches within the design process to facilitate the requirement of the physical growth in the local church.

1 > Design a facility without considering the concept of growth, whereby the church plants other churches.

2 > Consider the growth and expandability concept and design appropriately for future expansion.

The first such method is to design a physical facility to be a permanent worship facility. The worship facility is designed for a maximum number of parishioners and is designed as a static structure without the ability to expand. We have served many church clients that have set a particular target attendance whereby they would plant or mother another church within the community. Once the church meets this number of parishioners, the church makes plans to plant another church in another location within the community. This is a logical scriptural response to church growth.

We have had several church clients that have grown to maximum capacity and then multiplied the congregation to form additional churches to better serve the community in another geographical area. However, we have many clients that do not feel this addresses their particular vision for the congregation. This leads us the second approach to handling church growth, one which involves the architect.

The second approach to handling church growth within the physical church facilities is to provide a facility that is adaptable and flexible enough to easily be modified to handle additional numbers as the congregation grows.

PRE-PLANNING IS A PREREQUISITE FOR FLEXIBILITY...

In order for the architect to fully design for the concept of church growth, the initial planning process is critical. Architectural planning and programming is a process of thought and discovery that includes a "written program/plan" for the growth of the church. We often refer to this as pre-design services. The architect is instrumental in working with the building or planning committee of the church and will many times ask the following types of questions in order to better understand their needs:

> What type of additional space do you need for your present ministry needs?

> What type of additional space do you need for your short-range ministry needs (5-10 years)?

> What type of additional space do you need for your long-range ministry needs (15-20 years)?

> Does the church need to build another building, renovate the existing building or relocate?

> Is your current use of existing space efficient?

> Has the church set a realistic building budget, and can you afford what you currently need?

> Has a master plan been designed that will consider short-range as well as long-range goals?

The initial pre-design programming and planning process should ultimately develop a space analysis and program which lists each and every space that will be needed for the immediate needs. The architect will develop a database of needs. This database provides all the facts for the planning of the new facilities and should maintain a balance in all program areas including worship, evangelism, social and fellowship, education and administration. Proper pre-planning is a point of agreement for the present needs, short-term and long-term visions. The complete explanation of the spatial evaluation within the master plan process is covered within Chapter 4.

Proper pre-planning reinforces the confidence within the congregation by letting them know that the professional has adequately guided the building committee and leadership of the church in the long-range planning. He has assisted in quantifying the physical requirements of present and future needs to adequately house the vision and ministry

EXPANDABILITY AND ADAPTABILITY

of the church by both numbers of people and square footage. Proper planning establishes the credibility of committee members, church leadership and the pastoral team.

Proper planning will also include growth projections and a complete analysis of the existing space needs with the site. Proper pre-planning will evaluate the current site for overall capacity and ability to accommodate present and future growth. It has been our experience that a build-out sketch signifying the overall growth potential of a particular site is very valuable. It is not uncommon for a church to be sitting on 5, 10 or 15 acres of land with absolutely no idea of the maximum number of people the site will accommodate.

After the entire pre-planning and vision of the church has been well documented and analyzed through a proper space analysis and program, the architect is ready to translate this thought process into a design master plan fully addressing present needs and future growth. The process of developing a strategic master plan will indicate how large the church will ultimately grow numerically and how many people the site will accommodate. It will visually illustrate the expansion possibilities of the project.

Occasionally, growth projections for a growing church are not compatible with the current available land. It is not unusual for a church to have greater needs than a particular site can handle, and a decision must be made. The church architect may ask several questions:

SHOULD THE CHURCH BUY ADDITIONAL PROPERTY
AND FURTHER INVEST IN THEIR PRESENT SITE, OR DO THEY RELOCATE?

SHOULD THE CHURCH GO TO MULTIPLE SERVICES OR DO NOTHING AND
EFFECTIVELY STOP THE EVANGELISTIC MISSION OF THE CHURCH?

As the architect looks at short-term versus long-term needs, there are four typical design methods he may utilize in order to maximize the flexibility and adaptability of any sanctuary structure. Flexibility and adaptability are required if a physical sanctuary facility is to grow in size in order to accommodate increased numbers of a congregation over time.

These four methods will be described individually below:

METHOD I: INTERIOR MODIFICATION/EXPANSION

A sanctuary can be designed to allow for additional spaces such as classrooms, meeting rooms, etc. to take place directly adjacent to the worship space itself. These can be utilized simultaneously with worship, and when the time comes for the worship space to be enlarged, these classrooms are demolished by removing one or more walls. The sanctuary then expands into what once was already established interior space. Classrooms are then relocated.

This works best when the initial needs of a congregation include a small worship space with educational space. Therefore, the educational space can be built adjacent, alongside to or at the end of the worship space. It can be a fairly simple thing to remove a wall and expand the seating capacity at a later date. We refer to this as "interior expansion."

METHOD II: EXTERIOR EXPANSION

In this particular method, the overall design of the building is to allow for current needs of worshippers. However, the placement of that building on the site is critical due to the fact that the expansion for future growth will take place outside of the actual structure itself. Exterior expansion of a current existing worship facility will occur on the sides of the worship space or the end. The most expensive area within a worship space is the chancel area which includes the pulpit area, choir, orchestra (if the church so desires), baptismal room and dressing rooms. Therefore, the sanctuary is often designed with the chancel being fixed. This leaves the sides of the sanctuary or the end of the sanctuary for future expansion.

The master plan is critically important when this type of expansion is utilized. Outdoor space adjacent to the sanctuary must be sized and suitable for the proper expansion. Also, the walls and structure must be suitably designed to accommodate tear out and expansion at a later date.

It is critically important at this phase that the architect design not only phase one, but also have a conceptual design completed of phase 2 or 3 so that the building looks complete and whole aesthetically after the additions have been erected. You don't want a casual passer-by to drive by your facility and to be able to identify and count the building phases.

> YOU DON'T WANT A CASUAL PASSER-BY TO DRIVE BY YOUR FACILITY AND TO BE ABLE TO IDENTIFY AND COUNT THE BUILDING PHASES.

Curb appeal is always important, and it is critically important that the future phases accommodating the addition not violate the present design. It must work in harmony with it.

METHOD III: GOING UP WITH A BALCONY

It is possible to design a worship space to meet current needs and to accommodate a future expansion by adding a balcony. However, we have found that many times it is not the most economical method for expansion. Balcony space can be very expensive to construct because of several factors. Due to fire, safety and handicap access laws, it is no longer "cheaper to go up a second floor."

Staircase dimensions have been increased, and two sets of stairs are always required at a minimum. Handicap restrooms are required on each floor. Second floor loading requirements have increased substantially, and elevators are frequently required. There is a more expensive cost to the initial building due to the fact that the foundation structure for the future balcony must be installed during the initial phase of the project.

Though we have designed sanctuaries with balconies, we have found that they are most effective as a design solution when the site prohibits growth on the ground floor. On the other hand, as a worship space grows it is always a concern to minimize the distance between a pastor and the furthest most participant in the worship space. We like to keep this distance at 65 to 80 ft. at a maximum. Since this 'distance factor' is important, many times a balcony is the only way to keep this distance at a minimum, in a large church, by putting part of the congregation up over a portion of the first floor congregation in a raised balcony.

It should be noted that we have had many pastors over the last few years express a concern regarding balconies. In the event their services are evangelical and require participants to come from the worship space to the chancel regarding a salvation proclamation or to be prayed for at the conclusion of the service, a balcony is often viewed as an obstacle.

However, these are personal preferences and can best be discussed directly with an individual pastor, his leadership and the congregation.

...IT IS ALWAYS A CONCERN TO MINIMIZE THE DISTANCE BETWEEN A PASTOR AND THE FURTHEST MOST PARTICIPANT IN THE WORSHIP SPACE. WE LIKE TO KEEP THIS DISTANCE AT 65 TO 80 FT. AT A MAXIMUM.

METHOD IV: ADAPTIVE REUSE

Many times this method is not viewed as a direct possibility or potential in an expansion program of a local church. However to ignore it is a major fallacy in church design today. The above methods, I - III, allow for an expansion of 20% - 35% of the original worship size. Internal expansion allows for approximately 20% increase. External expansion can allow for as much as a 40% increase. A balcony will add 25% - 30% of the first floor capacity. However, in the event that a church views their long-term growth to be greater than these percentages, what is their option? Many times it can be this adaptive reuse concept.

Let's suppose that a church decides they need an initial sanctuary of 250 capacity. However, they have a long-range vision of a church with a capacity of approximately 700 - 800 people in the sanctuary for a single worship service. For personal reasons, they have decided not to use multiple services to accommodate growth for a long-term solution. They may attempt to provide double services only as they are building phase 2.

But how can a church worship space of 250 be expanded to 700 - 800 people? Both method I, II and III are highly unlikely as solutions to the problem. Therefore, why not address this design challenge in the following way:

1 > Design the initial worship space to be used as a worship space for the current phase only.

2 > When the church is ready for phase 2, the 700 to 800-seat sanctuary is built elsewhere on the site as the major sanctuary. The old sanctuary then becomes one of a number of typical uses:

> Fellowship Hall/Social Hall
> Wedding Chapel
> Mid Week Service and Prayer Chapel
> Subdivided for Christian Education
> Children's Church

Again, a complete space analysis, long-range planning and a master site plan is critical when approaching a project with this method. This is due to the fact that the location of the first building (which is now the sanctuary, but may later be a social hall) needs to be in such a position on the site that will work for both functions. The placement of that first building also must be compatible with the desirable location of the future sanctuary so that once all phases are built the building works in harmony.

SUMMARY

The above explanation of adaptability and flexibility of worship spaces is by no means inclusive of all ideas and concepts. However, it is a fairly complete review of planning concepts, which are important to understand in the long-range planning of church design concerning adaptability and flexibility. In any event, it is important to seek God for direction during all phases of your building program.

Consider the following scriptural directives:

"We should make plans...counting on God to direct us."
— Proverbs 16:9

"Carry out the plan in every detail, for it is the will of the Lord."
— I Chronicles 17:2

"Unless the Lord builds the house, its builders labor in vain."
— Psalms 127:1

In Proverbs, it tells us that where there is no vision, the people perish. Vision begins with the leadership of the local church. The architect can help prepare a long-range plan and space analysis program to provide the physical facilities, both now and in the future, to accommodate the vision for the church. A well-written plan for growth, adaptability and expandability is one that includes the needs of the congregation and balances them with a provision of resources and finances which are critical components of your long-range planning.

We understand that the facilities are merely tools of the ministry to help accomplish the ultimate vision and mission of the church; the building itself is not the church. However, we believe that we are to be good stewards in designing the physical facilities that house the church so that the church can be most efficient in reaching the lost souls of its community. Understanding the growth concepts of expandability and adaptability are critically important in the overall master planning of any church project. ∎

"

WE SHOULD MAKE PLANS...COUNTING ON GOD TO DIRECT US.
— PROVERBS 16:9

"

THE CONCEPT OF PARTNERING
Furthering the Kingdom through Teamwork

THE CONCEPT OF PARTNERING

The business world has always been a competitive and aggressive environment. Prior to the 1990's, the business world was not only extremely competitive, but there was an overriding sense that business rivals were in fact viewed as an enemy or an opponent. However, the 1990's seemed to usher in many different corporate concepts for the business world. One of these new concepts was the concept of partnering.

Gasoline companies partnered with fast-food restaurants. Pizza restaurants partnered with chicken restaurants. Even large corporations saw the advantages of partnering with one another. Various businesses that at one time considered each other enemy rivals, now saw the benefits of working together in a team atmosphere that was mutually beneficial to each partner. This shift in the business paradigm of 'business partners' or 'corporate association' even reached the age-old profession of architecture and construction.

Historically, the typical 'years-old' building delivery process, often referred to as 'design-bid-build,' has been patterned after the old concept of business. Contractors and architects were anything but allies. They often fought to control the domain of the owner's world and influence. Subcontractors and engineers battled through the building process inflicting wounds on each other as if this process was a combat war zone meant for fighting. Often the architect, builder, subcontractors and material suppliers were at each other's throat trying to limit their own liability, while at the same time trying to maintain their 'status quo' relationship on the building team. Often the owner was the loser.

The concept of teamwork and partnering not only affected corporate businesses in America throughout the 90's, but it also began to affect the way we viewed the typical building delivery process.

Could partnering be applied to the building delivery process in such a way to eliminate the costly finger-pointing, time delays and fighting among the key players in this process?

Could the client and owner of the building ultimately benefit from such a partnering process?

I believe that the answer is yes. Our experience with partnering has proved to be very successful and beneficial. Let's look at partnering and how this teamwork concept can be best applied to construction.

Partnering, within construction, often involves the development of a complete project team at the very beginning of any building project. The development of this project team can often take place prior to the architect actually beginning the design on the project. In other cases, the architect and the owner may actually select the contractor and other team players after the early preliminary design process has been completed. The complete project team (or partners) can consist of the owner, architect, consultants, interior designers, engineers, contractor, subcontractors and even material suppliers.

All are dedicated, from the very beginning, to the successful completion of the project. Each partner in turn benefits from the cooperative bond established between them, as well as the overall success of the actual project at hand.

KEY ELEMENTS IN PARTNERING
As with any business system or concept, there are some important factors

that must be in place in order for that system to operate effectively and efficiently. Likewise, in successful partnering there are several key elements that are necessary as follows:

Equity

All partners' interests in the team, including the project owner, must always be considered when establishing goals and project requirements. Each decision during the design process, construction document process and, ultimately, the actual construction process, must take into account the needs and provisions of all team members.

Goals/Objectives

The successful completion of any project is often due to a clear and concise development of goals and objectives for the project. The partners of the team work together to identify respective goals and needs for the project. Then the partnering team works together to develop a precise plan, direction and, ultimately, a design that benefits all the players and that fully meets the goals and objectives. Obviously, these goals include financial and budgetary goals of the owner.

Implementation

Partners work together to develop strategies for implementing the goals which are established.

Commitment

The successful participation of each partner cannot be dictated by the contract only. Success comes from personal and corporate commitment to the goals and objectives of the project.

Trust

Trust is the foundation of any partnering teamwork. It is of the utmost importance that the owner has confidence in the architect, engineer and contractor. It is also of utmost importance that each individual of the team has a confidence and trust in each of the other players, including the owner.

Timely responsiveness

Timely communication and decision making on a project not only saves money but also keeps problems from growing out of hand.

Continuous and ongoing evaluation

In order to ensure the success of a project, continuous evaluation of the goals and objectives are critical. Evaluation of the implementation strategies and time table of construction are also critical. All members of the team play an important role in this evaluation process.

Team synergy and interdependence

No longer are the architect and the contractor enemies of one another. No longer are the sub-contractors and the architect and engineers warring with one another. The consequence of all of the efforts of the team results in a unique interdependent relationship whereby all players sense the importance of their role in achieving the ultimate goal of the owner, which is the actual building of the project.

These are only a few of the major components found within a successful partnering process. However, one of the major areas receiving the most benefit of the 'partnering' process is the area of budgeting. Most all clients have a concern in the area of budgeting and financing. Let's review the actual budgeting and how partnering can solve many of the problems in the arena of project costing.

CONSTRUCTION BUDGETING

In the typical building delivery system process, the architect designs a building around the anticipated budget of the owner. Throughout the design process, construction cost can go up, budgets can be underestimated and the square footage of the building can grow. Often, expensive details can be designed into a building by the architectural team resulting in skyrocketing costs. Often the size of a project will grow, causing the final construction cost to exceed the original estimate. After months of work, the architect will ultimately complete the construction documents for the building.

At that point, when the construction documents are complete and approved by the owner, the drawings are usually printed and submitted to many different construction companies for pricing. Architects refer to this as the 'bid process.' Contractors will study the drawings and submit them to their building suppliers and sub-contractors. All of the components are then bid by the suppliers and subcontractors as they submit their costs to the general contractors. The general contractors will then compile their final prices and submit to the architect on 'bid day.'

When the final bid costs are submitted, it is not uncommon to hear of construction costs well over and above the original preliminary estimate which was analyzed months earlier. In fact, it is estimated that approximately 70% of all projects experience cost overruns of substantial proportions. This is an owner's worse nightmare. This causes construction delays, increased additional design costs and owner anxiety.

So what is the major difference between this typical "design-bid-build" building delivery system and the approach we use in partnering?

The significant difference between the concept of partnering and the typical construction delivery system is the opportunity for the complete team to work towards establishing a guaranteed maximum price during the initial design phase of the project. The contractor, playing his part on the team, is allowed the opportunity to share his expertise in the area of costing at a very early stage.

In the event that the needs or wishes of the owner exceed his initial budget, design changes can be implemented at an early stage, avoiding additional cost and delays. These changes can be made throughout the design process prior to the construction document phase. During partnering, the contractor's major sphere of responsibility, especially in the early phases, is cost consideration. This will assure the owner that he will ultimately get the building he wants, as defined by the goals and objectives, but at an agreed-upon cost and within his budget.

THE SIGNIFICANT DIFFERENCE BETWEEN THE CONCEPT OF PARTNERING AND THE TYPICAL CONSTRUCTION DELIVERY SYSTEM IS THE OPPORTUNITY FOR THE COMPLETE TEAM TO WORK TOWARDS ESTABLISHING A GUARANTEED MAXIMUM PRICE DURING THE INITIAL DESIGN PHASE OF THE PROJECT.

Partnering will also provide price-testing of multiple concepts prior to the completion of the actual design. This allows the owner and the architect a greater deal of design control as critical decisions concerning various concepts of the building can be based upon factual cost information and not speculative estimates. This team effort most always reduces construction cost on a project.

Perhaps the most unique valuable tool available to the partnering process during the entire design phase and construction document phase is "value engineering." Value engineering is a process whereby the architect and contractor can evaluate the project costs in an attempt to analyze various components and determine if there are any optional, cost-savings alternatives. Typically, value engineering on a bid project is applied only after the project comes in on bid day and is substantially over the owner's budget. However, this does not need to be the case.

In the partnering system, the entire team can evaluate the effect of alternatives on cost, time and quality of the building through a complete ongoing value engineering evaluation. The design, schedule, cost and quality of each project are unique to that project. The design is often a complicated process uniquely dictated by the owner's objectives, site characteristics, regulatory constraints and actual budgeting. A partnering team can best perform value engineering of the appropriate options during the design phase, prior to the preparation of the construction drawings.

PARTNERING BENEFITS

There are a variety of benefits to the owner, architect, engineer and contractor. Let us consider some of the major benefits:

Benefits to the owner:

> Reduced fees to the architect and engineering team
> Reduced exposure to litigation and disputes
> Reduced risk of cost overruns and delays
> Increased quality of the construction
> Accelerated schedule for building
> Efficient resolution of problems and issues
> Value engineering
> Improved constructability
> Increased opportunity for successful project

Benefits to the architect and engineer:

> Reduced liability for document deficiencies
> Enhanced role in decision making process
> Reduced administrative cost
> Lower risk of re-design due to cost overruns
> Increased opportunity for a successful project

Benefits to the contractor:

> Reduced exposure to litigation and disputes
> Increased productivity
> Expedited decision-making
> Opportunity to provide value engineering at an early stage

> Improved time management and cost control
> Less overhead and administrative costs
> Lower risk of re-design due to cost overruns
> Increased opportunity for a successful project

One major benefit of partnering for an owner is the possibility of fast-track construction scheduling. With the fast-track method, construction is started before the entire design and construction drawings are actually complete. This allows for the commencement of site work, foundation and the purchase of long lead items before the contract documents are actually finished. This often will offer one of the most valuable contributions of the partnering team effort.

Once the building footprint is complete, the architect and engineering team can complete the site plan and foundation design. While they complete the other aspects of the construction documents and detailing of the building, the contractor can apply for a building permit for the foundation and site development of the building. Once this permit has been released by the city, the contractor is free to begin construction while the architect completes the construction documents. This will often save 20% - 30% of the overall time on a project and expedite the move-in for the owner.

ONE MAJOR BENEFIT OF PARTNERING FOR AN OWNER IS THE POSSIBILITY OF FAST-TRACK CONSTRUCTION SCHEDULING.

OWNER CONTROL AND INVOLVEMENT

In the standard building delivery construction method, the contractor will bid out 90% -95% of the project construction to various subcontractors throughout the city. Unfortunately, the general contractor on the job does not always determine the successful completion or quality of the project. The final product and the quality of the ultimate building is often a reflection of the subcontractors utilized during the bid process.

In an attempt to keep costs low in order to receive the low bid award on the project, occasionally contractors will utilize extremely low bids from incompetent subcontractors or material suppliers. It only takes one incompetent major sub-contractor on the project to destroy the quality of the project. This can also affect the timely delivery of the project and the faith and trust of the owner with the architect and contractor team.

Many owners have only been exposed to the concept of bidding a project to several contractors for competitive pricing. However, in today's market the general contractor is many times not involved in the actual hands-on building during construction. He has become a specialized manager of construction and operates his business as a brokerage company with subcontractors supplying approximately 90 to 95% of the labor force of all trades on the project. Therefore, the successful completion of any project many times depends upon the subcontractors selected on a project during the bid phase. Contractors in any geographical area often will utilize similar subs for pricing on various projects.

The major variables between the low bid and other bids on any particular project are primarily found in only three areas:

1 > The actual subcontractors or material suppliers utilized on the project

2 > The overhead and profit percentage added on to the costs by the general contractor

3 > The contractor made a cost budget mistake

The overhead and profit on any particular job is often negotiable with the contractor at hand. The wrong subcontractor can produce catastrophic results on the construction site. Partnering often will provide a better delivery system than the typical "bid and build" due to the owner's involvement in the review of the final costs and in the review and approval of the selected subcontractors.

As the owner is looking for a contractor to become part of the team, it is important that the contractor be familiar with partnering. An overhead and profit will be established for the project prior to design. The contractor will be submitting his subcontract lists and bids for the original estimating of the building during the design phase. It is during these phases that trust between a contractor and the team is critically important.

Decisions can be made to include or to eliminate subcontractors from the preliminary design estimate in order to insure the quality of the building. With an open book policy, the sharing of precise line item costing can also be a benefit to the owner. With this type of partnering pricing, the owner has complete flexibility in reviewing construction costs and seeing where the money is going. This will often result in a trust factor that will continue throughout the entire project.

SUMMARY

Though many construction projects are still provided to owners throughout the country via the traditional bid and build delivery system, partnering is quickly gaining popularity with many owners, architects, engineers and contractors.

Many owners of projects currently being built by the design-bid-build process have simply not been introduced to the alternative approaches of delivery systems and have not been introduced to the advantages of partnering.

However, once an owner has been fully exposed to the advantages and has experienced the advantages of partnering on a project, they are most likely never to return to the traditional bid-build concept of delivery systems.

There is more time spent on the part of the owner prior to beginning the project with partnering due to the fact that the selection of the architect, engineer and contractor must be made very early. However, a unique bond of trust and camaraderie often builds amongst the team members through the process.

This will always lead to a successful delivery of a high-quality building.

Obviously, there will always be situations, especially in the government sector, where the traditional design-bid-build approach may be utilized. However, the concept of teamwork and partnering is certainly here to stay.■

EVALUATION OF YOUR EXISTING SPACES

Step-by-Step Worksheets

HOW TO EVALUATE

The initial phase towards successful master planning in the local church most always begins with the awareness of a physical need to accomplish an intended ministry. It often surfaces as a problem with the existing physical spaces of the church facilities. Therefore, one of the most important steps in the initial pre-planning phase is the evaluation of your existing spaces. There are questions that must be answered in order to evaluate such spaces.

1 > Does your facility adequately provide the spaces you need to fully accomplish your ministry objectives?

2 > Are the spaces adequately sized according to your need?

3 > Is your facility efficient in the use of the existing spaces?

4 > Are the spaces sufficiently heated and cooled to provide comfort?

This is not the assessment or appraisal of the physical building or the actual architecture, but the analysis of the actual spaces which is created by the physical architectural enclosure. The evaluation of the physical facilities of the architecture will be covered in Chapter 8.

This appraisal phase is in fact a self-evaluation of the spaces that house your current ministry. Often, this can best be accomplished by using worksheets that assist the building committee in this spatial assessment. Your church architect should assist you in this evaluation of space as the appraisal process will eventually help in the defining of your space problem and ultimately lead you towards the solution itself.

I find that by using a standard worksheet for this evaluation, the pastor or staff can better review their problem during a standard work week while at their church and then report to our office the following week.

The following is a worksheet that I use to assist our church clients in this spatial study. It is a very valuable tool in our evaluation phase of a church's spaces.

SPATIAL EVALUATION WORKSHEET

ATTENDANCE AND USE OF SPACE

Morning worship service(s)

NOTE: In the event that the church has more than one morning worship service, please list all services.

Current Attendance for Sunday Morning Worship:

High attendance   _____   during the past year
Low attendance   _____   during the past year
Average per Sunday   _____   during the past year

Past Sunday Morning Worship Attendance Record:

Average worship attendance one year ago   _____

Average worship attendance two years ago   _____

Average worship attendance five years ago   _____

Average worship attendance ten years ago   _____

Is your current worship space adequate on Sunday?
[ ] yes [ ] no

Sunday Evening and Mid-Week Service Attendance

Sunday evening worship service average attendance _____

Mid-week worship service attendance _____

List Additional Uses of Your Facility: Maximum Attendance:

_____   _____

_____   _____

_____   _____

_____   _____

Worship Space and Seating

The present worship space is:
[ ] A permanent worship auditorium
[ ] An interim worship auditorium
[ ] Other, describe _____

List the other uses for that space: _____
_____

Worship Seating Capacity

Pews (main floor)   _____
Choir   _____
Balcony   _____
Extra Chairs   _____
Worship Seating Total: _____

Seating Arrangement

Pews (main floor) back-to-back row spacing _____ (in.)

Seat width per person _____ (in.)

List aisle widths
  main _____   side _____ (in.)

Does your current seating arrangement work? [ ] yes [ ] no

Choir Seating Types

[ ] Pews
[ ] Stack chairs
[ ] Folding chairs

Choir, back-to-back spacing _____ (in.)
Seat width _____ (in.)

CHANCEL AND PULPIT (PLATFORM)

Depth of existing chancel   _____ (ft.)

Width of existing chancel   _____ (ft.)

Height above main floor _____ (ft.) Number of steps _____

Distance from the front of the platform to the first row of seats
  _____ (ft.)

Is the distance from front of pulpit platform to first row of seats suitable
for your church? [ ] yes [ ] no

If not, why? _____

Is pastor's access from study convenient and desirable?
[ ] yes [ ] no

If not, why? _____

LORD'S SUPPER TABLE

Table size _____ (length and width)

Clearance to first row of seating   _____ (in.)
Clearance behind   _____ (in.)
Clearance to sides   _____

Is the communion table elevated? [ ] yes [ ] no

List the height above floor: _____ (in.)

Does your communion space work well for your worship service?
[ ] yes [ ] no

If not, why? _____

BAPTISMAL

Does your church use a font for sprinkling? [ ] yes [ ] no

If so, answer the following questions:

If you use a font, is the current one appropriate? [ ] yes [ ] no

Describe the appropriate location of the font in your worship space.
_____
_____
_____

Does your church use a tank for immersion? [ ] yes [ ] no

If so, answer the following questions

Existing Tank size:
Width _____ (ft./in.)
Length _____ (ft./in.)
Depth _____ (ft./in.)
Water depth _____ (ft./in.)

Is a glass viewing provided? [ ] yes [ ] no

If so, list the size of glass _____ x _____ (in.)

Is a glass viewing needed? [ ] yes [ ] no

Do you currently have baptismal dressing room provisions?
 [ ] yes [ ] no

Are they adequate? [ ] yes [ ] no

Size _____ x _____ (ft./in.)

Do you use individual booths? [ ] yes [ ] no

Do you have storage for robes? [ ] yes [ ] no

Do you have toilets in the dressing areas? [ ] yes [ ] no

ORGAN AND PIANO

Piano information
Age in years _____ (ft./in.)
Size-Length _____ (ft./in.)
Width _____ (ft./in.)
Height _____ (ft./in.)

Is the piano and the space for it adequate? [ ] yes [ ] no

Pipe organ information

Is capacity satisfactory for auditorium? [ ] yes [ ] no

Electronic organ information

Organ console
Width   _____ (ft./in.)
Depth   _____ (ft./in.)
Height   _____ (ft./in.)

Is the capacity satisfactory for your worship space?
[ ] yes [ ] no

Do you use instruments for your worship service?
[ ] yes [ ] no

Is the chancel space sufficient for the instruments and musicians?
[ ] yes [ ] no

VESTIBULE AND OTHER ROOMS

Is the major vestibule/foyer large enough? [ ] yes [ ] no

Is the vestibule accessible from both the educational building and worship? [ ] yes [ ] no

Is the vestibule convenient to parking areas? [ ] yes [ ] no

Is the vestibule visible from street and/or drive approaches?
[ ] yes   [ ] no

Are there enough entrance and exit doors? [ ] yes [ ] no

Are they well located? [ ] yes [ ] no

Do they swing outward in accordance with the building code?
[ ] yes [ ] no

Are they equipped with panic hardware devices? [ ] yes [ ] no

Is the entire entrance area inviting to the public? [ ] yes [ ] no

Is the entrance area attractive? [ ] yes [ ] no

CHRISTIAN EDUCATION

Do you have effective spaces for the nursery? [ ] yes [ ] no

Describe: _____
_____

Do you have effective spaces for your children's Christian Education
program? [ ] yes [ ] no

Describe: _____
_____

Do you have effective spaces for your Youth program?
[ ] yes [ ] no
Describe: _____
_____

Do you have effective spaces for your adult's Christian Education
program? [ ] yes [ ] no

Describe: _____
_____

Are there sufficient Christian Education offices? [ ] yes [ ] no

Describe: _____
_____

Are there sufficient Christian Education resource rooms?
[ ] yes [ ] no

Describe: _____
_____

OTHER SUPPORT SPACES

Do you have usable janitor closets? [ ] yes [ ] no

Do you have effective HVAC and electrical rooms?
[ ] yes [ ] no

Describe: _____
_____

Do you have effective storage areas for each ministry?
[ ] yes [ ] no

Describe: _____
_____

Do you have effective lockup rooms or a safe for finances (after the offering)? [ ] yes [ ] no

Describe: _____
_____

Do you have effective outside storage spaces for yard equipment?
[ ] yes [ ] no

Describe: _____
_____

Do you have sufficient administrative spaces for the pastor and all of his staff? [ ] yes [ ] no

Describe: _____

_____

Do you have sufficient miscellaneous space such as ushers' room, flower preparation room, Lord's Supper preparation room?
[ ] yes [ ] no

Describe: _____

_____

SUMMARY

It is of the utmost importance to always evaluate your existing space conditions prior to beginning the planning process for the next phase.

In fact, both the church designer and church client often experience this self-evaluation phase to be very enlightening. Perhaps one of the most valuable tasks during the pre-planning phase is this spatial evaluation.

The church architect can be very instrumental in assisting the church in this evaluation. A healthy inward-focused evaluation will result in a healthier approach during the problem-solving phase. This will result in a better and more responsive design solution for your next building project.■

EVALUATION OF YOUR PHYSICAL FACILITIES 8
Does Your Building Need Work?

LET'S LOOK AT YOUR BUILDING...

As a church grows, ministry needs grow. The growth of ministry in a local church often expresses itself through space problems. The space issues can be addressed and evaluated as we discussed in the previous chapter.

However, as a church building ages, there can be various issues that arise regarding the physical components of the building. There can be failures in the roofing, failures in the mechanical and electrical components of the building and failures in the structural components as well.

It is important to evaluate the existing condition of your buildings prior to beginning the master planning process. In the event that there are problems within your existing building structure, the architect will need to be apprised of this situation. In the event that there are substantial problems within your existing physical facilities, the architect will need to evaluate the situation as it relates to the final master plan.

It may require some demolition of portions of the building or it may require extensive renovation. The architect can advise the church and assist in this physical evaluation of the facilities.

The following worksheets can assist the church in communicating with your architect:

PHYSICAL FACILITY EVALUATION WORKSHEET

STRUCTURE AND CONDITION OF BUILDING

Year erected   _____

Age of structure   _____

Date of last repairs   _____

List all of the repairs over the last 10 years: _____
_____
_____

Date of last redecoration (painting, wall papering, etc.): _____
_____

What was done? (describe) _____
_____
_____
_____

Lighting system: describe the effectiveness of the following lighting systems:

Pulpit   _____
Choir   _____
Pews   _____
Balcony   _____
Area under balcony   _____

Light source is
[ ] Direct
[ ] Indirect
[ ] Chandeliers
[ ] Other _____

Do your currently have dimmers connected to your lighting?
[ ] yes [ ] no

Describe: _____

Describe your needs regarding the lighting system:
_____
_____
_____

Describe your needs regarding the heating and air conditioning system:
_____
_____

Are your worship space acoustics satisfactory for music?
[ ] yes [ ] no

Does your building have an echo? [ ] yes [ ] no

Describe the echo: _____

Does the sound system work? [ ] yes [ ] no

Sound system consultant or supplier is: _____
_____

Recording capability? _____

Microphone locations _____

Is there an intercom system? [ ] yes [ ] no

Location of stations _____
_____

Is a projector system needed? [ ] yes [ ] no

Is a rear-projection system needed? [ ] yes [ ] no

Is computer wiring needed? [ ] yes [ ] no

Is an acoustical consultant needed? [ ] yes [ ] no

Is there an existing Radio and TV broadcast provision?
[ ] yes [ ] no

Sight lines — do all seats have a satisfactory view of all service and
program activity areas? [ ] yes [ ] no

Do certain seating locations have sight line difficulties?
[ ] yes [ ] no

Locate and describe problem: _____
_____
_____
_____

Is modification required in your building? [ ] yes [ ] no

If yes, describe work needed: _____
_____
_____
_____
_____

Describe floor construction and condition: _____
_____
_____
_____
_____

Describe wall construction and condition:

(exterior) _____
_____
_____

(interior) _____
_____
_____
_____

Describe any maintenance or repairs needed: _____
_____

Describe any needed alterations: _____
_____
_____
_____

Condition of windows
[ ] Good
[ ] Fair
[ ] Poor

Describe maintenance, repairs, or alterations needed: _____
_____
_____
_____

Describe the ceiling condition:
[ ] Good
[ ] Fair
[ ] Poor

Describe appearance: _____
_____
_____

Describe maintenance, repairs, or changes needed: _____
_____
_____

Describe the existing roof structure:
[ ] Laminated wood
[ ] Wood trusses
[ ] Steel trusses
[ ] Wood rafters
[ ] Other (describe): _____
_____

Condition of roof structure (describe): _____
_____
_____

Roofing material _____ condition _____

How old is the existing roofing? _____

_____

Describe needed repairs: _____

_____

_____

Redecoration of existing auditorium needed (describe extent):

_____

_____

SUMMARY

Once the physical facility of the building has been evaluated, the architect will have a better understanding of the needs for renovation or alteration. In the event that any substantial renovation or even demolition is required, the architect can include such work in the master planning and construction costs during the early planning stage.■

SPACE ANALYSIS OF FUTURE NEEDS 9
Your Plan for the Future

LOOKING AT YOUR NEEDS

Once the church architect has evaluated your existing spaces and your existing facilities, it is now important to evaluate your ministry need. As we discussed in Chapter 2, "What is Church Master Planning?", the architect can study your ministry needs and reflect such needs in a space analysis. The space analysis is a program that lists all spaces needed by the church.

Each and every space needs to be identified and listed along with the occupant count and a corresponding square footage. The church architect, working closely with the church building committee, can study the ministry needs and use various tools to survey the existing needs and to convey them to both the church and the design department of the architectural firm.

Our design firm uses two types of forms to assist in the study of space requirements. The first set of forms are worksheets used to analyze the individual space needed in various department areas of the church. I refer to these as "Spatial Needs Worksheets."

The second set of documents is the "Space Analysis and Program" form. This is a form which we use to adequately document the space needs and communicate the space needs back to the church building committee. This form is used as a tally sheet to analyze and add up the various spaces within the new complex. The final result of this worksheet is an individual listing of all required spaces with corresponding area calculations and an accumulative summary of the entire complex.

SPATIAL NEEDS WORKSHEETS

The following "Spatial Needs Worksheets" assists the church in identifying specific needs within various departments in the church. These worksheets will help the church identify and itemize spatial needs in the following areas:

> Church Administration Department
> Preschool Christian Education
> School-Age Christian Education
> Youth Christian Education
> Adult Christian Education
> Social Hall and Kitchen Needs

A building committee can work directly with the church architect by filling out the various sheets within this chapter. These will help develop the number of rooms needed in the various departments, the capacity per room and in some cases, the actual square footage required for the space.

The church planner can take this information and insert it into the "Space Analysis and Program" to determine the final size of the facility. Let's review these spatial needs worksheets. They are typically broken down and isolated by department.

EACH AND EVERY SPACE NEEDS TO BE IDENTIFIED AND LISTED ALONG WITH THE OCCUPANT COUNT AND A CORRESPONDING SQUARE FOOTAGE.

CHURCH ADMINISTRATION WORKSHEET

	Existing (sq. ft.)	Required (sq. ft.)	Proposed Space	
			Immediate	Long-Range
Reception		300		
Pastor's office		250		
Pastor's Study		200		
Minister of _____		160		
Minister of _____		160		
Minister of _____		140		
Administrator		140		
Pastor's secretary		150		
Other Secretaries		100		

Recommendations:

Existing office should be
[ ] Remodeled   [ ] Expanded   [ ] Converted

Describe:_____

List your offices needed according to their priority:
1 > _____
2 > _____
3 > _____
4 > _____
5 > _____

CHRISTIAN EDUCATION PROGRAM

PRESCHOOL DIVISION WORKSHEET

Organization		Current Attendance	Expected 5 years enroll | attend		10 years enroll | attend	
Sunday Morning Sunday School	Ages					
	Infant					
	1					
	2					
	3					
	4					
	5					
TOTAL						
Mid-Week Church Training	Infant					
	1					
	2					
	3					
	4					
	5					
TOTAL						

List existing and needed furnishings: _____
_____
_____

List special needs (such as restroom accessible nearby): _____
_____
_____
_____

CHRISTIAN EDUCATION PROGRAM

CHILDREN'S DIVISION WORKSHEET

Organization		Current Attendance	Expected 5 years enroll | attend		10 years enroll | attend	
Sunday Morning Sunday School	Ages					
	6					
	7					
	8					
	9					
	10					
	11					
TOTAL						
Mid-Week Church Training	6					
	7					
	8					
	9					
	10					
	11					
TOTAL						

List existing and needed furnishings: _____
_____
_____

List special needs (such as restroom accessible nearby from corridor):
_____
_____

CHRISTIAN EDUCATION PROGRAM

YOUTH DIVISION WORKSHEET

Organization		Current Attendance	Expected 5 years enroll | attend		10 years enroll | attend	
Sunday Morning Sunday School	Ages					
	12					
	13					
	14					
	15					
	16					
	17					
TOTAL						
Mid-Week Church Training	12					
	13					
	14					
	15					
	16					
	17					
TOTAL						

List existing and needed furnishings: _____
_____
_____

List special needs (such as restroom accessible nearby from corridor):
_____
_____

CHRISTIAN EDUCATION PROGRAM

ADULT DIVISION WORKSHEET

Organization		Current Attendance	Expected 5 years enroll | attend		10 years enroll | attend	
Sunday Morning Sunday School	Depts.					
TOTAL						
Mid–Week Church Training						
TOTAL						

List existing and needed furnishings: _____

_____

_____

List special needs (such as restroom accessible nearby from corridor):

_____

_____

SPACE EXISTING AND NEEDED - ADULT DIVISION

| | NOW | | NEEDED | | | |
| | | | In 5 Years | | In 10 Years | |
	# Cl.	Total sq. ft.	# Cl.	Total sq. ft.	# Cl.	Total sq. ft.
Young Single						
Young Married						
30-59						
60 & up						
Misc.						

On previous chart, circle ages now in same department rooms.

Calculate needed space for maximum attendance based on 70% - 80% of expected enrollment (See chart "Determining Space in Age Division Rooms" for recommended area per person).

List existing and needed furnishings. Give an approximate cost figure for additional furnishings.
$_____

List special needs: _____
_____
_____

CHURCH KITCHEN WORKSHEET

Church's Use of Kitchen		Immediate Needs	Long-Range Needs
Meals	No. Served		
	Frequency of Use		
Menu	Preparation		
	Cooking		
	Baking		
	Warming		
	Refrigeration		
	Freezing		
Operation	Complete Preparation		
	Limited Preparation		
	Brought from Home		
Serving	Buffet		
	Cafeteria		
	Banquet		

SIZE DINING AREA NEEDED	Immediate Needs	Long-Range Needs
Number of People to Be Served		
Sq. ft. area		

SPACE ANALYSIS AND PROGRAM

Once the church building committee and the architect have analyzed the individual needs in the worksheets above, they are now ready to compile all of their needs into this space analysis and program worksheet. This will begin to define the overall size of the entire complex.

The following is an example of the program we utilize to assist our church clients in this phase:

THIS IS A MASTER PLAN GUIDE LISTING MOST OF THE TYPICAL SPACES AND CONCERNS COMMONLY FOUND WITHIN CHURCH DESIGN. ITS USE IS FOR YOU TO FILL IN THE BLANKS AND TO MODIFY IT TO BEST REFLECT YOUR INDIVIDUAL NEEDS. ONLY CONCERN YOURSELF WITH THE CAPACITY OF SPACES IN NUMBERS OF PERSONS. WE WILL ASSIST YOU IN CONVERTING THESE FIGURES TO SQUARE FOOTAGES AND THEN TO CONSTRUCTION DOLLARS FOR PRELIMINARY ANALYSIS.

NOTE: PLEASE FILL OUT THIS FORM FOR IMMEDIATE NEEDS, FUTURE NEEDS (5-10 YEARS) AND LONG-RANGE NEEDS (20+ YEARS). THIS WILL ALLOW US THE OPPORTUNITY TO VIEW ALL NEEDS AS WE PLAN TOGETHER FOR THE CHURCH'S MASTER PLAN.

CHURCH NAME_____

SPACE NAME	PEOPLE COUNT	TOTAL SQ. FOOTAGE
1 > WORSHIP		
Sanctuary		
First Floor Seating		
Seats or Pews		
Balcony		
Flat Floor or Sloped Floor		

Space Analysis and Program cont.

SPACE NAME	PEOPLE COUNT	TOTAL SQ. FOOTAGE
Area for Ministry		
Chancel Sized for Plays, Adaptable		
Expandable		
Parking Ratio (list)		
Handicap Seating Areas		
Hearing/Sight/Disabled Area		
Additional Support Facilities		
Choir		
Orchestra		
Pipe Organ		
Multi-Media, Rear Projections, Etc.		
Video/Audio		
Location		
Prayer Rooms		
Baptismal Pool and Dressing Rooms		
Fonts & Locations		
Counseling Rooms at Front		
Choir Room Near Choir Area		
Minister's Lounge/Prayer Area		
Rooms for Ministry at Front		
Communication Area & Table		
Lobby		
1 SF Per Person Minimum		
User-Friendly Information Booth		
Toilets Near		
Coat Area		
Usher's Room		
Bride's Room		
Bookstore		
Storage Area for Chairs, Etc.		
Coffee Area		

Space Analysis and Program cont.

SPACE NAME	PEOPLE COUNT	TOTAL SQ. FOOTAGE
Misc. Spaces		
Halls & Walls		
Mechanical/Electrical Rooms		
Janitor's Closet		
SUBTOTAL FOR WORSHIP AREA		
2 > ADMINISTRATION SPACES		
Offices		
Reception and Seating		
Central Secretaries		
Pastor's Office		
Assoc. Pastor's		
Administrator		
Treasurer's Room		
General Offices / List #		
Conference Room		
Counseling Center		
Work Room / Printing		
Storage		
Toilets		
Conference Room		
Print Room		
Misc. Spaces		
Halls & Walls		
Mechanical/Electrical Rooms		
Janitor's Closet		
SUBTOTAL FOR ADMINISTRATION AREAS		
3 > CHRISTIAN EDUCATION		
Children's Church		
Seating		
Type of Worship		
Puppets/Multi-Media		
Storage Room		

Space Analysis and Program cont.

SPACE NAME	PEOPLE COUNT	TOTAL SQ. FOOTAGE
Sunday School Classes (List Number)		
SS Class		
SS Class		
SS Class		
SS Class		
SS Class		
SS Class		
Misc. Spaces		
Halls & Walls		
Mechanical/Electrical Rooms		
Janitor's Closet		
SUBTOTAL FOR CHRISTIAN ED. AREAS		
4 > FAMILY LIFE CENTER		
Gym Type Space		
Kitchen		
Storage		
Vestibule		
Game Room		
Toilets & Lockers		
Showers		
Offices		
Storage for Sports Equipment		
Misc. Spaces		
Halls & Walls		
Mechanical/Electrical Rooms		
Janitor's Closet		
SUBTOTAL FOR FAMILY LIFE CENTER		
5 > MISCELLANEOUS ROOMS/SPACES		
List by Name		
_____		
_____		
_____		

Space Analysis and Program cont.

SPACE NAME	PEOPLE COUNT	TOTAL SQ. FOOTAGE
5 > MISCELLANEOUS ROOMS/SPACES cont.		
_____		
_____		
_____		
_____		
_____		
SUBTOTAL FOR 1 — 5		
6 > DESIGN CONTINGENCY		
_____		
_____		
_____		
_____		
_____		
GRAND TOTAL		

SUMMARY

Once your church architect has provided the assistance to walk you through this "Space Analysis and Program" worksheet, the church will better understand the entire scope of their ministry needs. By applying appropriate construction cost numbers, the architect can provide the church with an "Opinion of Construction Cost."

The church can then compare the projected cost of the project with their available funds to determine if they can afford the project. If funds fall short of the final construction costing, the architect may need to utilize some type of phasing for the project. ■

GUIDELINES FOR PROPER PLANNING
Rules of Thumb

10

WHAT IS A RULE OF THUMB?

Many times during the pre-planning design process, it may be important for the church architect to make certain planning assumptions regarding the new project. Several issues may need to be addressed during this pre-planning phase as follows:

> Acreage needed for expansion
> Approximate size of the expansion
> Parking required for proper planning
> Preliminary budget costs of expansion
> Analysis of need

Obviously, these issues will ultimately require the extensive planning expertise of the church architect. However, the initial application of these various 'rules of thumb' make it possible for the planner to address some of these issues very early in the design process without expending a lot of time and effort.

What exactly is a 'rule of thumb' in church design?

A 'rule of thumb' is a general principle, standard or ruling guide that can be applied in similar situations regarding church planning in order for the church planner to arrive at a preparatory analysis of a planning situation early in the pre-planning phase of design.

These rules of thumb are useful only in making approximations and should never be used for final planning. However, they can be extremely valuable in their use as early planning guidelines for the church architect and planner. Rules of thumb are used primarily for estimation of property, building space and other needs pre-requisite to the actual planning process.

SITE PLANNING

Required Acreage and Parking Needs: For early planning purposes, the church should use the following ratios to figure the required acreage for auditorium, educational buildings, and parking:

Minimum Needs

PARKING: Minimum parking (1 car per 4 people)
(Always refer to local building codes.)
WORSHIP: Figure two acres per 300 in worship attendance

When parking is based on zoning ordinances of a city municipality, the parking plan is most always undersized. Most municipalities require one car per 4 - 5 people in attendance. However, we have found the following ratios are best suited for the growing church.

More Appropriate Planning Ratios

PARKING: Maximum parking: (1 car per 2.5 people)
WORSHIP: Figure three acres per 300 in worship attendance
An additional 2 - 4 acres may be needed for activity buildings such as family life centers, gymnasiums and outdoor recreation areas. (See the parking section below under "Building area and ground footprint.")

Parsonage

Occasionally, the pastor's home is located on the site and called either a parsonage or rectory. However, the tendency recently is to locate the pastor's home off-site. Typically, nowadays, the pastor's home should not be on the church building site. Many pastors now own their own home. However, if the parsonage is located on the church property, the planner should add at least one-half acre of land for it.

Site Designing with Utilities: In the early design phase of a church project, the architect is to give special attention to various utility-type concerns as follows:

> HVAC condensing units
> Drain pipes and drainage
> Retention ponds
> Off site drainage
> Electrical service
> Water and sewage availability
> Garbage and waste disposal
> Chimney design and layouts
> Grates and pipes

REQUIRED AREA AND BUILDING FOOTPRINT
WORSHIP SPACE GROUND COVERAGE

Seating Capacity

The actual square footage required for the worship space seating itself may only be 7 - 9 square ft. per person depending on the design of the space and on the location and spacing layout of the seating or pews.

However, for preliminary analysis, the following ratios can be utilized for establishing the overall footprint of the worship space, which includes the chancel and entry lobby.

Seating Capacity	Sq. Ft. Per Person
Up to 200	16 -18
200-500	13 -16
600 - 1,000	11 -14
1,000 and up	10 -12

Educational Building

For the entire Christian Education building, the church planner should initially plan for 35 - 45 square ft. floor space per person.

A larger church with extensive educational programs, including departmental meeting rooms may require up to 50 - 60 square ft. per person.

For initial planning and layout purposes, a desirable width for most small education buildings is 45 ft. - 55 ft.. Suitable and efficient structural components can easily span the roof without interior columns. Desirable widths for larger buildings are more in the range of 60 ft. - 70 ft.

Activity Building/Family Life Center

Depending on the actual needs of this building, the planner can plan for approximately 35 - 40 square ft. floor space per person.

If a high school regulation gym is planned, the size is 50 ft. x 84 ft. from outside line to outside line. Plan for at least 5 ft.- 6 ft. of aisle around the court for the out-of-bounds area. In the event that the gym/family life center is to also serve as a temporary worship space, one can figure on an approximate seating capacity of around 600 people within the gym space.

Parking Layouts

This is an area that can really confuse the typical site planner that is not familiar with church planning. Most city zoning requirements establish ratios that require a minimum number of parked cars for a church building. These minimum ratio requirements vary from city to city.

However, most cities have requirements such as 1 car per 4 seats or 1 car per 5 seats. However, the real-life ratio is closer to the following ratio: Figure one car for every 2 - 3 auditorium seats. A planner can often estimate, for preliminary planning, the following ratios:

Figure 85 - 110 cars per acre.

An average is 100 cars per acre.

The following ratios can be used to determine the area needed per car:

Parking Angle	Need	Drive
90	350 Sq. Ft.	(2-way drive)
60	400 Sq. Ft	(2-way drive)
45	450 Sq. Ft	(2-way drive)

Obviously, the final need for parking area should always be determined by your church architect during the site planning process. The number of non-parking driveways and drive aisles can also affect the above numbers.

Shared Parking: Look for opportunities to share parking with neighbors such as banks, schools or shopping centers. This can reduce site development costs.

WORSHIP SPACE PLANNING

The worship space within the church should always be the central focus of the architecture. It is the one central large space within the plan that allows for the entire congregation to join together to praise and worship their God and listen to the preaching of the Word. Though the entire worship space should be designed by the church architect, there are a variety of guidelines that can allow for some preliminary planning by the church building committee during the pre-planning phase. These can ultimately assist the church planner in determining space requirements.

Pulpit Platform & Chancel Area

Minimum Platform size: The space for the pulpit platform from the front to back is at least 8 ft. minimum. For larger buildings, the planner should figure at least 12 ft. - 20 ft.. The space required is dictated by the function of the platform. Many churches are beginning to use larger stages to accommodate orchestras, plays and pageants.

Pulpit platform height: The chancel is often raised for the purpose of providing proper lines of sight from all of the seating. The actual height varies depending on the size and shape of the sanctuary space. Preliminary planning can suggest from 3 ft. - 4 ft..

In very small buildings with less than 10 or 12 rows of pews, the planner should suggest 1 ft. - 18 in. in height. Appropriate steps from the platform to the nave floor are important.

Pulpit to first pew space: The planner should figure 6 ft. as a minimum. Often 8 ft. - 10 ft. is more appropriate for early planning. In the event that the Lord's Supper table platform is included or that ministry (i.e. prayer for individuals after the service) is utilized by the church, 10 ft. - 12 ft. may be better.

In an Episcopal Church where the Eucharist table is paramount and central to the liturgical planning, the church planner should figure appropriate space for kneeling and movement.

Platform Floor: Always design the floor for sufficient loading. Attempt to use 2 layers of 3/4 in. tongue and groove plywood with suitable metal floor framing to eliminate any bounce. It is also appropriate to glue and screw the plywood to the framing below.

The floor of the platform should be built with a lip on the forward edge in order to assist the carpet installer in hiding the seam of the carpet.

The entire floor should be carpeted with the exception of the actual choir area, which could be a hard surface to facilitate in the acoustics.

Choir Area

Choir capacity: Figure the following for early planning:

> Choir capacity for smaller church (200 – 500)
> > 8% - 12% of worship capacity

> Choir capacity for larger church (500 – 1,000)
> > 6% - 8% of worship capacity

The individual choir rows should be at least 3 ft. 0 in. wide. However, for easier movement between the aisles, figure 3 ft. 4 in. to 3 ft. 6 in. for both the chair and the aisle.

The planner should figure 20 in. - 24 in. per person for movable choir type chairs.

Baptistery

The sizes of the various tanks on the market vary but consider the following sizes for preliminary planning:

> Size of the interior tank is 4 ft. x 6 ft. minimum inside tank, 4 ft. x 7 ft. 3 1/2 in. maximum.

> Overall size (steps both ends) 4 ft. 6 in. x 12 ft. 9 in. minimum, 4 ft. 9 in. x 18 ft. maximum.

Typical water depth is 3 ft. without glass and 3 ft. 6 in. with glass.

Locate the actual baptistery floor at least 2 ft. above the last row of the choir. It is often desirable to raise the tank floor higher than 2 ft. 0 in. for maximum visibility. Design it for maximum visibility, accessibility and convenience. Remember that the baptistery service is a worship experience as well as a community celebration.

CONGREGATION SEATING

Pew or seating spacing
Spacing of the seats or pews is 36 in. minimum back-to-back. If dancing or additional movement is required, figure a minimum of 42 in. spacing for each pew.

Maximum pew length
Figure seating for 12 - 14 people.

Seating Capacity for pews
Though the pew companies often figure 20 in. per person, the minimum spacing figure should be 24 in. per person, with total pew capacity figured on a pew-by-pew basis rather than an accumulative additive sum of all the linear footage of the pews. The accumulative method provides unrealistic pew seating capacities and calculations.

Aisles
Main aisle width should be a 4 ft. minimum with a 6 ft. - 8 ft. preferable. Side aisles should never be less than 3 ft. 6 in. minimum to accommodate both the parishioner and the handicap.

The last pew should never be placed on the rear wall, though that was a typical norm many years back. Always allow at least 4 ft. 0 in. at a minimum between the last pew and the rear wall. Depending on the overall size of the sanctuary, this distance could be much larger to accommodate the crowd.

Never face the seating directly to large sun-lit windows that can blind and distract from the worship experience.

Avoid designing the seating with dead-end rows of seating that abut exterior or interior walls. Always leave a cross-aisle of sufficient width at the rear of the sanctuary.

VESTIBULE/LOBBY

The vestibule space of years ago was often considered an air-lock entry only. It was usually treated as a necessary space waster. However, this is not the case today. Many churches utilize this space for a variety of uses. The space becomes an ideal area for fellowship and lingering, both before and after the service. The planner should allow at least the following ratio for pre-planning:

> 1.5 sq. ft. - 3.0 sq. ft. per person in worship space

The lobby and entrances to the auditorium should be large enough to be convenient for all weddings, funeral services and special events. Seldom will the lobby ever be designed too large.

THE LOBBY AND ENTRANCES TO THE AUDITORIUM SHOULD BE LARGE ENOUGH TO BE CONVENIENT FOR ALL WEDDINGS, FUNERAL SERVICES AND SPECIAL EVENTS. SELDOM WILL THE LOBBY EVER BE DESIGNED TOO LARGE.

Intimacy

The lobby and entrance should give a feeling of intimacy by using appropriate lighting, ceiling height, plants, furnishings, etc. The visitor should always be able to step out of the flow of the foyer to be greeted without creating a bottleneck in the traffic. The design of the entry of the building must communicate a "you are welcome" attitude to the visitor.

Security

Always consider the concept of security when designing the exterior components of the building near the entrances. The placement of the building entries should relate visually to the approaching streets, parking and approach. Appropriate exterior lighting is the best all around deterrent regarding security issues. Motion sensors can be utilized to control lighting at various areas of the building.

Consider the following security measures:

> Shrubbery should never hide windows, entries or doorways
> Fire exit-only doors should not have hardware on the exterior

> All entrances should be visible to the approaching police
or security vehicle

Balcony

The capacity of any balcony is usually 25% - 40% of the main floor seating. The actual design of the balcony is a specialized area and therefore, simple guidelines are difficult to establish for this area. For appropriate sight lines to floor at front edge of pulpit platform, the planner must usually provide a minimum of 45 ft. - 55 ft. from the front of the balcony to the front edge of the pulpit platform.

THE ULTIMATE COST OF A BALCONY OFTEN WELL-EXCEEDS THE COST OF PROVIDING THE SEATING ON THE MAIN FLOOR

The ultimate cost of a balcony often well-exceeds the cost of providing the seating on the main floor when one considers the additional costs of the following:

> Additional cost of second floor structure (especially if the structure is cantilevered)

> Cost of stair access

> Costs of meeting the ADA (Americans with Disabilities Act), i.e. elevators, etc.

It is our experience that balconies tend to produce church spectators. The local church desires the parishioner to be a participant rather than a spectator. A balcony seating capacity should never exceed 40% - 50% of the first floor capacity.

Exception

Many larger sanctuaries are now being designed with modified balconies that begin at the ground floor of the sanctuary and slope upwards until it meets with the second floor area. These can be extremely effective when designing a large church with limited ground area and whereby a design objective is to minimize the distance from the pastor and the furthest parishioner.

Steeple

The typical height of a steeple is most often figured as a distance equal to the roof eave to ground level as a minimum. The maximum is figured as the distance equal from the roof ridge to ground level or a factor of 1.5 times that distance if the overall design of the sanctuary can adequately accommodate a high steeple within the design.

Heating and Cooling

Plan heating and cooling in zones with separate temperature controls. Locate ducts some distance away from the worship space to reduce the distraction of the noise. Use sound-lined ducts with vibration isolators to reduce potential noise problems.

Electrical and Lighting

Use natural lighting coming from the out-of-doors as much as practical. Be careful with natural light coming into the sanctuary from behind the chancel, as this can create difficult problems. Sound and lighting controls should be in the sanctuary rather than in a separate space.

Consider the following lighting levels for preliminary planning:

Auditorium Lighting (general)	30 — 45 ft. candles
Choir	40 — 50 ft. candles
Accent Lighting (chancel)	85 — 100 ft. candles
Wall Sconces (specialty)	10 — 15 ft. candles
Foyer (soft and concealed)	10 — 20 ft. candles

Lights under the balcony should always be recessed and flush mounted.

AUDIO-VISUAL DESIGN

Controls

Locate all audio controls in a protected environment, located within the auditorium. Never locate behind a window or in a separate room.

Projection screen

Locate a concealed screen. Size (width) to be approximately 1/5 to 1/6 of the distance from the screen to the furthest viewer. Keep the nearest viewer approximately 3 times the screen width from the front of the screen.

Audio

Invest in an audio consultant to assist the architect. It is better to have a lively auditorium rather than a dead one. Materials such as drapes or acoustical panels can be installed to improve sound quality.

> Microphone jacks should be installed for the pulpit, choir, the Lord's Table baptistery, organ, piano, specialty instruments, etc.

> Always provide conduits underground and overhead for necessary speaker wires and other uses.

CHRISTIAN EDUCATION SPACE

In the Christian Educational building, there are a variety of guidelines that can assist the church planner in anticipating the size of the space required for the ministry needs. The following are some standard rules of thumb for pre-planning:

CHRISTIAN EDUCATION SPATIAL NEEDS

	Ages	Suggested Numbers per Room	Floor Space per Classroom	
			Classroom Min	Classroom Max
Preschool	Infant	12	20 sq. ft.	35 sq. ft.
	Toddlers	12		
	2	15		
	3	15		
	4	15		
	5	15		
Children	6 - 8	15	20 sq. ft.	20 sq. ft.
	9 - 11	15		
Youth	12 - 18	30	10 sq. ft.	20 sq. ft.
Adult	19 & Up	40	8 sq. ft.	15 sq. ft.

PRESCHOOL

Space per person: Overall, the planner should figure 35 sq. ft. per person for the entire building. In no case should a number less then 20 sq. ft. per person be used.

Minimum room size: Figure at least 250 sq. ft.

Individual room capacities for preschool:

Ages	Capacity
K, 1	5 - 8
2, 3	10 - 12
4, 5	12 - 16

Individual room capacities for children
> Space per person: 25 sq. ft. recommended, 20 sq. ft. minimum.
> Room capacity: 14 - 16 children
> Room proportions: Always try to utilize a 2/3 ratio for width to length.

Individual room capacities for youth
Classrooms: 15 sq. ft. recommended, 12 sq. ft. minimum.

Individual room capacities for adults
Classrooms: 12 sq. ft. recommended, 8 sq. ft. minimum.

WEEKDAY PROGRAMS

Daycare and kindergarten
35 sq. ft. per person minimum, or as required by codes.
Play yard: 50 sq. ft. per child minimum.

General requirements
It is often wise to eliminate bearing walls if possible. This will allow for greater flexibility in the future as ministry needs change.

The educational portion of the building should be designed with a minimum of second floor or roof bearing walls, if possible, to add to greater flexibility. Obviously, this is not always possible.

ASSOCIATED SPACES

ADMINISTRATIVE
Pastor's study
250 - 350 sq. ft. recommended; 200sq. ft. minimum.

Privacy for counseling
In many cases, the Pastor may want his study or counseling rooms designed with a private entrance so people may come and go without traveling through the reception area of the offices.

Staff members' offices
120 - 180 sq. ft. recommended; 120 sq. ft. minimum.

MUSIC

Rehearsal room
15 sq. ft. per person.

Robing rooms
4 - 6 sq. ft. per person.

Instrumental rehearsing groups
15 sq. ft. per person.

Handbell rehearsing room
10 sq. ft. per person.

MEDIA LIBRARY

Size
2 sq. ft. per person in education program recommended.

DINING AND FELLOWSHIP

Capacity for dining
1/3 worship capacity minimum, 1/2 worship capacity recommended.

Dining space
12 sq. ft. per person at tables recommended, figure at least 15 sq. ft. per person for round banquet type seating.

Kitchen size should be 1/4 of the size of dining area.

ACTIVITY, FAMILY LIFE, OR RECREATION BUILDING

High school regulation basketball court size
50 ft. x 84 ft. plus 6 ft. area around court.

Ceiling height
20 ft. minimum: 24 ft. − 26 ft. desirable.

Room size
60 ft. x 100 ft. plus ft. per row of bleachers seating.

Game rooms
40 ft. x 60 ft. desirable.

Crafts rooms
16 ft. x 24 ft. minimum.

Group meeting rooms
14 ft. x 20 ft. minimum.

CHAPEL
Seating capacity can vary, but is usually at least 50 - 175 people @ 15 sq. ft. per person.

Bride's dressing room
12' x 12' recommended; 8' x 10' minimum.

OUTDOOR RECREATION
Varies depending on the needs.
RESTROOMS
Minimum Fixtures: Meet current code. Most codes require 1 stall per 50 women and 1 stall per 100 men of the worship space.

MECHANICAL AND EQUIPMENT ROOMS
Small buildings up to 5,000 sq. ft.: 1% - 1 1/2% of total building space.
Above 8,000 sq. ft.: 2% of building space.

HANDICAPPED

General Requirements
Always refer to local codes.

Building access
No steps between parking lot, entrance to the building and building interior.

HALLS AND WALLS
Approximately 8% - 12% of the entire space should be allocated for halls and walls. Included within this estimate would be appropriate space for duct and pipe chases.

FINANCING CONCEPTS
There are various financing formulas, which can be used for preliminary financial planning. These will be more fully discussed in Chapter 11.

The following formulas are often used for pre-planning of funding capacity:

1 > Three times the annual income of proceeding year.

2 > Figure approximately 25% - 35% of annual income to go toward debt retirement.

Many churches will employ a professional fund-raiser to assist in the raising of the funds for construction. The fee for such a service varies from company to company. In many denominations, there is a fund-raising program that can be used for financing. In any event, most professional fund-raisers advertise that they can typically raise 1.5 - 2.2 times the annual budget over a three year fund-raising program.

Concerning the cost of the project, most churches look primarily towards the construction cost. However, there is a significant difference between the construction cost of the building and the final total project cost of the project.

The experienced church architect should have the experience to assist you in the financial phases by helping to establish the various additional costs often associated in the total project cost. The total project budget must be established early for proper cost considerations.
The total Project Budget is often comprised of the following:

TASKS	OTHER COSTS
Construction Cost	$ VARIES
Architect & Engineering	8% -14% of Construction Cost
Testing and other fees	½%- 1% of Construction Cost
Construction loan costs	6% -10% of Construction Cost
Financing closing costs	4% - 7% of Construction Cost
Contingency	3% - 5% of Construction Cost
Furnishings	6% -10% of Construction Cost
Landscape	4% -10% of Construction Cost

TOTAL PROJECT COST EVALUATION

Construction cost is often only 70% - 80% of the total project cost. Another way to state this formula is the following:

The project cost is 1.2 to 1.25 times the construction cost.

> NOTE: The above 'Rules-of-Thumb' are to be used only for preliminary planning and are not to take the place of appropriate professional architectural consulting and planning.■

THERE IS A SIGNIFICANT DIFFERENCE BETWEEN THE CONSTRUCTION COST OF THE BUILDING AND THE FINAL TOTAL PROJECT COST OF THE PROJECT.

FINANCIAL CONSIDERATIONS
Counting the Cost

THE COST FACTOR

Several years ago, I remember sitting in a church builder's conference that was supported by a particular denomination in my state of Virginia. We had discussed aspects of building one floor versus two floors during the morning session. The afternoon seminar was focusing on building problems and it was titled, "Church Building: A Common Denominator of Failure."

The title of that particular seminar caught my attention. What could be a common denominator of failure amongst building projects for the local church?

> Could it be a failure to unite the people in one accord?
> Would it be the difficulty of selecting the right architect or the right contractor for the project?
> Could it possibly be zeroing in on the exact mission and ministry for the church?

Or perhaps a common problem would be improper master planning and accounting for growth over the next several years. I was certainly surprised when the leader of that particular seminar answered the question. Exactly what is a common denominator of failure when it comes to the local church building program?

"

THE MAJOR COMMON DENOMINATOR OF FAILURE AMONG CHURCH PROJECTS IS THE INABILITY TO COUNT THE COST AND PROJECT THE ENTIRE PROJECT COST AT AN EARLY ENOUGH PHASE IN THE TOTAL PROJECT. TOO MANY PROJECTS RUN THOUSANDS OF DOLLARS OVER BUDGET, PUTTING THE PASTOR AND THE CHURCH'S MINISTRY IN JEOPARDY.

"

I was really surprised. Now I knew that many architects have problems with construction cost estimates. And I also knew that construction cost often has a tendency to creep upwards through the design process. Nevertheless, I was shocked to find out that the major problem that many churches face is the cost estimating and analysis portion of the master plan.

The speaker went on to say, "In fact, approximately 80% of churches today struggle with the construction cost and budgeting aspects of their project."

Eighty percent! It was shocking.

How could the design profession and the construction profession so fail the local church? As I reflected on past projects (not our own) in my own community, it became obvious that the problem was prevalent. A recent elementary school went over budget by 25%. A library exceeded its budget by 35%. A city hall building far exceeded the budget estimates, and the city was unable to fund the newly proposed project.

A church client had recently come into my office with a horror story regarding his project. Apparently, this particular church had an approved budget by their board and their financing institution of approximately

EXACTLY WHAT IS A COMMON DENOMINATOR OF FAILURE WHEN IT COMES TO THE LOCAL CHURCH BUILDING PROGRAM?

$1 million. The contract with their architect was for 10% of the low bid. Preliminary plans were drawn up and approved by the church. Renderings of those plans were placed in the vestibule, and everyone was excited to begin the drawings and construct the building.

The church had high hopes that the entire project could be built for approximately $1 million. The construction drawings were complete and the project was bid out to several contractors. The low bid of the entire project was $1.4 million. The high bid was $1.8 million. It was shocking as I listened to this church's story. The architectural firm had missed the overall budget by 40% - 80%. The church could no longer afford the project and the pastor was forlorn.

When this sort of thing happens, it is damaging to the church. But the damage goes well beyond the mere absence of a building. The credibility of the pastoral staff, board and leadership is at risk.

The story in this true-life example gets worse.

As I listened to the pastor share his heart with me, he continued to discuss the architectural proposal and contract which the church had approved. The contract required that the church pay the architect a fee of 10% of the low bid. They anticipated that the low bid would be approximately $1 million, making the fee approximately $100,000. However, at the end of the bid process, the church received a bill for $140,000, exceeding their architectural fee budget by $40,000. The architect had billed the church for 10% of the low bid, which was $1,400,000. The church was shocked and I was shocked as well.

I remember looking into the sad eyes of the pastor as I explained to him our major objective at this point...

> It was not to build a building instantly.
> It was not to design another edifice immediately.

Our major objective and goal was to re-group, re-count the cost, re-evaluate their situation and put together a project that would not exceed their budget, thus reinforcing and re-establishing the credibility of their leadership in the eyes of the church. That is exactly what we did.

The cost factor, without question, is one of the most challenging aspects of the master plan and building process for the local church. Most churches are not prepared to deal with the budgeting issues, let alone the banking issues and the ultimate financial considerations and concerns that must be addressed. Unfortunately, many architects are not prepared to provide the church with adequate budgeting in order to make the process an easier one.

As I sat in that seminar and listened to story after story of churches that were hurt due to poor budgetary planning. I remember praying to the Lord:

> *"Oh, Lord, please give us the wisdom to know how to step up to the plate and accept the challenge of effectively dealing with the financial considerations and concerns of building projects for the local church. If you but give us this wisdom, we will serve you with all of our soul, strength and might."*

We have now designed some 300 church projects, and I am grateful to say that the Lord has indeed given us the wisdom to approach this entire financial and budgeting challenge. A project can be financially evaluated in such a way that maintains the credibility of the leadership, allowing churches to build without going into extreme financial debt.

In this chapter, we will look at several concepts. We will look at what the Bible has to say about finances, and more specifically, what the Bible has to say about financial aspects of building. We will address the entire issue of counting the construction cost. We will illustrate to you the difference between the project budgets and the construction cost budgets, which is often the arena whereby the financial aspects of a church project goes awry.

We will also assist in helping you address the financial capability question. We will discuss church financing, the types of financing and ideas regarding fund-raising. We have been very fortunate to have been able to put together a unique approach to costing that addresses these issues effectively and allows the church architect to count the cost early in order to avoid financial pitfalls for the church he is serving.

THOUGHTS FROM THE WORD

There are a variety of scriptures and Biblical concepts throughout the Word of God that can be applied to the financial considerations of building the local church. Let us consider a number of scriptures regarding financial matters and explore how these Biblical concepts can be applied to the financial arena of the church building project.

He will prosper us...

"Then he answered them and said unto them, 'The God of heaven, He will prosper us; therefore we His servants will arise and build.'"
— Nehemiah 2:20

As Nehemiah reflected on the challenge ahead of him regarding the rebuilding of the walls of Jerusalem, he knew that he could not do it alone. Nehemiah did not have the resources, the strength or the power to rebuild the walls of the great city of God. However, there is one thing that Nehemiah did have. Nehemiah had the faith in his God of heaven. Nehemiah was able to grasp hold of the fact that it is God that builds the walls. The finances and the resources were completely beyond his grasp. However, Nehemiah did know one thing, and that was "The God of heaven, He will prosper us..."

One of the first financial considerations and Biblical concepts that must be understood and grasped by the local church and their leadership is the entire concept that God can and will prosper you. If you are walking in His truth and in His will and need additional physical facilities in order to accomplish your ministry goals, God will prosper you.

If you have caught the vision of the Lord regarding that which He would have you build, you can know that God will prosper you. The church's job is to believe that. Your job is to embrace that, internalize it and hang your hat of faith upon it. Nehemiah's response to the fact that God would prosper them was quite simple. They would arise and build. We discussed this in Chapter 3. It is God's responsibility to provide the financial resources, and He often uses His people to provide such finances. Then, it is our responsibility to arise and build.

Proper stewardship...
King Solomon certainly understood the power and the truth behind these words that he penned. It was King Solomon that built the great temple of Solomon that we discussed in Chapter 3. It was King Solomon and his father before him, King David, that honored the Lord with their wealth.

HONOR THE LORD WITH YOUR WEALTH, WITH THE FIRST FRUITS OF ALL YOUR CROPS; THEN YOUR BARNS WILL BE FILLED OVERFLOWING AND YOUR VATS WILL BRIM OVER WITH NEW WINE.
— PROVERBS 3:9-10

Solomon asked for wisdom and the Lord bestowed upon King Solomon and the entire kingdom a tremendous multitude of blessings, including an overflowing of financial blessings.

Another critical Biblical truth that must be understood if we are to properly enter into this financial arena of master planning and building is the entire concept of stewardship. Though it is true that the Lord will provide the financial prosperity that is needed for your building as he did in the

TOO MANY CHRISTIANS AS WELL AS BOARD MEMBERS AND BUILDING COMMITTEE MEMBERS ARE STRESSED OUT REGARDING THE FINANCIAL CAPABILITY OF THE CHURCH AND YET AT THE SAME TIME ARE NOT HONORING THE LORD WITH THE FIRST FRUITS OF THEIR OWN FINANCIAL BLESSINGS.

days of Nehemiah, it is also important to realize that he works through you and me. The Lord expects us to honor Him with our wealth and then with the first fruits of the crops. Too many Christians as well as board members and building committee members are stressed out regarding the financial capability of the church and yet at the same time are not honoring the Lord with the first fruits of their own financial blessings. I have discussed this concept with many members of many building committees over the last 20 years. I have often broached the entire concept of stewardship and financial accountability regarding our first fruits. It is really surprising to me how few people understand this entire spiritual truth.

As with many scriptural directives in the word of God, this comes with a promise. It is very simple. Solomon states that if we honor the Lord with a portion of that which He has blessed us with (the first fruits), "then our barns will be filled overflowing and our vats will brim over with new wine." God promises us His blessings. In the local church today, if the individual members of the church practiced this principle of honoring the Lord with our first fruits, then our barns would be filled to overflowing. If our barns were filled overflowing, there would never be a financial need in the local church today. The concept of stewardship and accountability is critical in the local church as we approach this entire arena of financial and budgeting considerations for the building program.

My particular church recently had a capital campaign. The slogan of that campaign was very simple...

"Equal sacrifice, not equal gifts."

It is not uncommon for a pastor or a building committee member to share with me that they are resting the future of their entire building program on the backs of one or two wealthy businessmen within their congregation. Now this is not to say that we shouldn't be grateful for those businessmen that God leads to us in the local church.

Nevertheless, I do not believe that it was ever God's intention for one or two people to carry the majority of any building campaign in the local church. "Equal sacrifice, not equal gifts," is a strong statement when it comes to financial accountability, regardless of the income bracket.

It really doesn't matter whether a particular individual in the church receives a six-figure or seven-figure income or whether it's a poor widow on a meager pension. God's truth has always been firm regarding the widow, the widow's mite, the loaves and the fishes. It was once estimated that if the poor widow's mite had been saved and deposited by the temple in the "First City Bank of God, Jerusalem" (drawing approximately 4% interest semi-annually from some certificate of deposit or mutual fund) actual temple fund today from that mere widow's mite would exceed $4,800,000,000,000,000,000,000,000.00.

❝ EQUAL SACRIFICE, NOT EQUAL GIFTS. ❞

I don't know about you, but that's more money than I can conceive. If a simple bank on earth could multiply the meager gift of the poor widow's mite to such an astronomical financial figure, just consider what treasures this beautiful, dedicated, widowed, old woman has in heaven today where "moth and rust does not corrupt."

Perhaps stewardship is one of the most important concepts for the church to consider and to communicate to their people regarding the financial considerations of the building project.

GENEROSITY LEADS TO THANKSGIVING...

"Now he who supplies seed to the sower and bread for food will also supply and increase your store of seed and will enlarge the harvest of your righteousness. You will be made rich in every way so that you can be generous on every occasion and through us your generosity will result in thanksgiving to God."
— II Corinthians 9:10

Several years ago, a pastor phoned me and asked me to come and discuss the financial considerations, budgeting and fund-raising for his particular project. His church was a young, growing church and the pastor was attempting to build his first building. Our preliminary estimates revealed that the project would be somewhere between $3 million and $3.5 million dollars. This was no small undertaking for this church.

I drove across the city, pulled into the church's parking lot and found my way into his office. We opened with prayer and then he looked deep into my eyes. "Michael," he said, "I believe God wants my people to be blessed by raising the money for this project as we go. I believe that the Lord spoke to my heart and told me that He would turn the hearts of the fathers to the children. I believe that God will use the fathers to raise this financing to build this first project. I've decided not to speak to a bank at this time, but I will share with the fathers what the Lord has shared with me."

Then his unique request came. He continued, "Michael, I need you to find me a contractor that would be willing to build this project for me without our church having money in the bank."

I watched and listened carefully as reports came in of the generous ways in which the church fathers began to give towards the project. Their generosity resulted in thanksgiving, and the church grew and continues to grow to this day. Consider this scripture again:

"You will be made rich in every way so that you can be generous on every occasion and through us your generosity will result in thanksgiving to God."

It is important for the church to understand that it is God that makes us rich in every way. The Lord will bless us abundantly in order for us to provide for His kingdom. In fact, the major reason the Lord blesses us is so that we might give to others.

I visualize this biblical principal as a large funnel. The Lord pours blessing into my funnel from heaven. Now these blessings are not always financial. They may be blessings of wisdom and health, as well as generosity. I often imagine the Lord coming down with his large hands and wrapping around the funnel of my life and directing the end of the funnel to that which He would have blessed through me. Through our generosity, there is tremendous thanksgiving to God.

I watched as the fathers gave to this church program, and I watched as they made their monthly payments out of the cash they had raised. The Lord continued to bless them in every way. In fact, they experienced directly what Matthew spoke about regarding "give and it shall be given unto you." We will never 'out-give' God. We as people of God must practice generosity. By practicing generosity, we will be made rich in every way, and the result will be not only the physical kingdom and spiritual kingdom of God being enlarged in our communities, but it will also result in a tremendous outpouring of thanksgiving to God Himself from whom all blessings flow.

COUNTING THE COST EARLY...

"Suppose one of you wants to build a tower. Will he not first sit down and estimate the cost to see if he has enough money to complete it? For if he lays the foundation and is not able to finish it, everyone who sees it will ridicule him saying, 'This fellow began to build and was not able to finish.'"
— Luke 14:28

Common sense will often teach us that we are not to begin any work without first investigating to see if we have the resources to complete that work. If any of us would begin the construction of a house for our families on a small residential side street, we would be expected to complete that house. In the event that we built the house and was never able to complete the roof, we would be the ridicule of all our friends.

This story, told by our Lord, really represents the absurdity of those individuals that might decide to become disciples of Jesus without really counting the cost and considering the difficulties which they might face in the end. In reality, and in the truest sense of the word, Jesus is making that argument. Perhaps the price will most always bear scrutiny. The Lord would suggest to us regarding our spiritual life that we are to count the cost, lay a deep foundation upon the solid rock which is Jesus and then reach high into heaven. Though the most fully accurate evaluation of that scripture suggests that Jesus was specifically talking to us about our Christian life, the very concept of counting the cost, during a building project, is an important one and has direct ramifications on the building campaign of the local church.

Remember the story that I told you in the beginning of the chapter regarding the state church building conference that I attended years ago? You might recall that I said that over 80% of church projects have budgetary problems. In most all of these cases, the church did not count the cost. I have heard the sad stories of numerous projects where "counting the cost" early was a complete failure. This would often result in the waste of serious church time, resources and finances. Ultimately, the construction drawings would be completed only to be filed away in storage bins of some local architectural firm never to be built.

Over the years, numerous millions of dollars have been invested in plans that cannot be built because the cost was never counted. In fact, in my particular state, there was a local church not long ago that never counted the cost. The foundation of the building was completed. The concrete block walls of the building began to reach up to the sky and the project stopped. The roof structure was delivered to the project and sat alongside the project. Another successful battle raged by the spiritual enemy of our souls and the church, and a project halted because no one counted the cost.

In Luke 14, Jesus asked this question, and let me paraphrase, "If one of you are going to build a tower, why would you not first sit down and estimate the cost to see if you have enough money to complete it?" It is critical in today's society that we count the cost early. Counting the cost is not a popular task, and, in fact, is not a task that is successfully accomplished on many projects.

One only needs to read the news section of your city newspaper to see project after project that has experienced the "construction cost creep" to the extent that the final construction of the project can cost thousands, and sometimes millions, of dollars more than the original estimate. In some cases, it's not that the planners, architects and contractors didn't count the cost; they did not count the cost successfully.

> ...HE MOST OFTEN WILL LOSE A DEGREE OF CREDIBILITY REGARDING HIS ABILITY TO LEAD SPIRITUALLY.

The Lord says that if you lay the foundation and are not able to finish your project, everyone that sees it will ridicule you. In relationship to the church, it is the leadership of the church that is ridiculed. Oh, of course, the church members and the other members of your community may not verbalize this ridicule to your face. However, credibility will be lost.

When the credibility of leadership is lost, it is a sad and fearful thing. Trust is a difficult thing to regain once it is lost. This affects not only the physical building program of the church but often results in having a catastrophic effect on the spiritual aspects of the church as well. If a pastor loses credibility in a building project, he most often will lose a degree of credibility regarding his ability to lead spiritually.

There are many churches throughout America today that are suffering from the blight of never "counting the cost." Sure, their buildings may have been completed, but they are half full. The roof structure may have been installed, but the hearts of the people have been stretched and stressed. The building may be occupied by a number of members, but the debt service on the mortgage loan to cover the expense of the building drives the church and steals from ministry programs long forgotten.

I recently read that when the debt service of a mortgage loan drives the ministry of a local church, the life expectancy of that pastor seldom exceeds a couple of years. What a sad and dreadful thing for a building program. What should be a blessing to the local church when facilitating their ministry, becomes a weight and a burden on the shoulders of the church to bear.

God is telling us through this verse that we are to accurately project the entire cost of not only the building but also the entire project early in the programming process. It is critically important. If the actual construction cost and budgetary parameters are not defined until late in the building program, you too will become a statistic and will join the large mass of 80% of churches whereby financial considerations become an ultimate problem in your building project. With God's help and by applying the Biblical principles above, you can overcome.

COUNTING THE CONSTRUCTION COST

As illustrated by our discussion and review of Luke 14:28 above, it is critical that the church architect and planner have experience in counting the construction cost early. It is important to determine accurate costs for a project. I believe it would be safe to say that on most projects, someone attempts to determine some type of construction costs. In fact, on many projects, a construction cost may even be determined somewhat early in the entire process.

If this is the case, then why do so many churches experience catastrophic failures when it comes to appropriate budgeting and construction costing? The answer to that question is really quite simple.

The early costs are incorrect.

It is important that the church planner address the construction cost and concerns by addressing with the committee several major determining factors :

    1 > The actual size of the facility

2 > The architectural design of the building
3 > The construction methodologies and materials utilized
4 > The construction climate in the community
5 > Site development costs

There may be a multitude of additional factors that ultimately determine the final construction cost of any facility. However, the above five factors tend to be the most critical parameters that can be modified, evaluated, and manipulated in order to anticipate and control the ultimate construction cost of the project.

It is important that the architect determine the size of the building based on the program and the ministry needs of your church. It is also important to begin discussing, at an early stage, the entire concept of budgeting as well. The architect should be able to manipulate the above five factors to suitably bring the project in sight of the proposed budget for the church. The design might be a very simple wood frame, wood truss structure. It might be a very large glass, crystal-like cathedral. The design of the actual building and the methodologies and materials utilized in the building can be critical.

It is also important to review the building climate of the particular community. In a case where the building industry is down, construction costs can come down as many contractors compete for the projects that are available. However, as I am writing this book, our particular financial and building climate in my city is such that contractors are extremely busy. Construction costs have gone up by 15% - 20%. The effect of the construction cost in this arena has absolutely nothing to do with the size or the design of the building. But the architect must take this into account. Many times the construction cost of the building can exceed the client's budget due to the site considerations of the project. A parking lot, the entrance, requirements from the city regarding the actual site plan, asphalting of the site, concrete curb and gutters, water hook-ups, electrical hook-ups, sanitary sewer and storm drains, retention ponds, storm water management as well as sewage pump stations all can account for anywhere between 15% - 25% of the entire project.

A church building of approximately 1,000 seats will require parking of 300 - 400 cars. Depending on the site, the cost of a typical space to park those cars can range between $1,200 - $1,500 per car. Four-hundred cars in a particular parking lot at $1,500 per car equates to $600,000 alone. In many cases, as I have evaluated construction costs of other projects that cannot be built due to excessive costs, it is the site cost itself that has drastically exceeded the budget and halted an otherwise successful building project.

It is very important that the church architect and planner count the construction cost early by evaluating the size of the building, the actual architectural design of the structure, the construction methodologies to be used, the climate of the construction industry in the particular community as well as the site development issues early in the process.

There are many methodologies that architects can utilize to assist the owner in counting the construction cost early. It is my experience that most architectural designers will tend to estimate the cost based on a square foot number pulled out of a current cost construction manual. At best, the estimates will allow the client to determine a construction cost that may only be as close to 20% or 30% (if that good) from the final cost. Historically, architect's estimates have been 20% - 25% short of the ultimate construction cost. There are a number of reliable sources that can be utilized today by architects in order to arrive at a more reliable construction cost early in the process.

Three sources that can be utilized to evaluate construction cost at a very early phase are as follows:

F. W. Dodge, McGraw-Hill cost information systems, 1221 Avenue of the Americas, New York, NY 10020
Telephone number: 609-426-7311

R. S. Means, P.O. Box 800, Kingston, MA 02364
Telephone number: 617-747-1270

Guidelines, Box 456, Orinda, CA 94563
Telephone number: 800-634-7779

Guidelines, Means and F. W. Dodge all research appropriate construction cost from coast to coast and communicate it via reports, seminars, workbooks and published manuals for architects to use. Though we have utilized all three of these in the past, we recognize that though they are reliable sources, they are not the best source for us to determine construction cost.

Though these cost manuals are available for architects to use, I find that the most reliable source that we can use in counting the cost early is historic data. We work with contractors on a weekly basis pricing out churches that we design. We track the construction cost of the building, the site and the complete development of the project. We will also track the square foot cost of the mechanical systems, plumbing systems, electrical systems, carpet, etc. Ultimately, this has provided our office with a tremendous historical tool and database which becomes very effective in projecting costs for churches.

Many years ago, the only building delivery system that was available for the architect and the owner was the traditional design-bid-build process. This traditional process which has been perpetuated by architects for many years involves the architect playing the lead throughout the entire design process. The architect begins the design process and then completes the construction drawings prior to turning to his construction company allies in his particular area. The construction cost estimate is basically a square foot estimate prepared by the architect at the early phase and could ultimately be as much as 20% - 45% below budget.

During this type of building delivery process, preliminary drawings are completed, construction drawings are drawn and the owner pays the majority of the architect's fees out prior to any real final pricing. Then the entire set of construction documents, including the construction plans and the book specifications, are given out to individual contractors to price. In most cases, the architect has been involved with the owner for 6 - 8 months at the time when the contractor is first brought in to price the project. It's not surprising to find that the construction cost can often exceed the architect's estimate by 25% - 40%. It is exactly this reason why so many churches find themselves in a financial predicament and become prey to the typical "budget crisis" that tends to attack the local church during the building process.

Over the last many years, many corporations have begun exploring the entire concept of "partnering." It's not uncommon to drive down the street and to see a sub-sandwich store partnering with a gasoline station in the same facility. While visiting one of our churches in a rural community, I pulled into what appeared to be a gasoline station. However, it was more than a typical gasoline station, as the gas company had "partnered" with a hamburger chain. I gassed up my Ford at the Amoco station and caught lunch at the Burger King. Amoco and Burger King had partnered together to the mutual benefit of the both of them.

It is anticipated by many "in the know" throughout the construction industry that the traditional design-bid-build process just does not work any more. If this old traditional delivery system process does not work, then why does it continue to perpetuate itself in the market place?

Simple.

Most government agencies utilize this procedure in order to eliminate and minimize kickbacks on their projects. In other cases, clients literally think

FINANCIAL CONSIDERATIONS

167

that the only method to arrive at competitive construction costs is to bid the project out to several contractors well after the construction documents have been completed. But the timing for 'counting the cost' is wrong as it is too late in the process. As we explored in the book of Luke, the Lord Jesus Christ said to count the cost early. Who would build a tower that would not first count the cost?

We have been very successful in exploring the concept of partnering earlier in this book. This entire concept of partnering is discussed thoroughly in Chapter 6, "The Concept of Partnering, Furthering the Kingdom through Teamwork."

So, how does partnering and 'counting the cost' go hand-in-hand? We like to establish the entire team early. We feel that the right contractor on the team is a tremendous advantage and plays an advantageous role in cost accountability. We like to explore this entire concept of partnering with the church and then assist them as they interview contractors to be brought onto the team.

It is not uncommon for one of our churches to interview three or four contractors and then ultimately decide on one contractor to be utilized as a team player. Obviously, there are no contracts signed at that point between the owner and contractor due to the fact that no construction numbers have yet been established. It's an absolute no-risk, no-commitment and no-cost adventure for the local church. The contractor becomes part of the team and begins to exercise his expertise throughout the process in establishing cost numbers from the very early stages of the project.

Remember the pastor in the earlier portions of this chapter that phoned my office regarding building his first $3 million project on a cash basis? It was critically important for us to establish a true construction cost early on that project and to be accountable to such. We assisted the owner in interviewing several contractors and ultimately agreed upon one. As we worked through the preliminary design of the project, the contractor worked hand-in-hand with us addressing the financial considerations and budgetary costs of each item throughout the architectural design.

The preliminary and the construction cost budget estimate that we prepared for the owner was not an estimate pulled out of any manual. The preliminary cost that we projected was not a square foot analysis provided by an architect out of touch with construction costs in today's society. It was a combination of professional efforts and expertise combining the architectural designer with the constructor of the project, thus arriving at a true construction cost analysis of the entire project. Our preliminary cost estimates projected the building to cost $3,000,000.00. Once the owner approved the preliminary budget and the preliminary plans, we proceeded with the construction drawings. To provide for cost accountability on the part of our office, the construction drawings were printed out of the computer every two weeks and provided to the partnering contractor for review.

THE CONTRACTOR BECOMES PART OF THE TEAM
AND BEGINS TO EXERCISE HIS EXPERTISE THROUGHOUT THE PROCESS IN ESTABLISHING COST NUMBERS FROM THE VERY EARLY STAGES OF THE PROJECT.

In this way, we as architectural church designers were able to stay accountable to the budget that had been presented to the church. Once the construction drawings were complete, the owner signed a contract for the same construction dollar amount which was previously given to him in the preliminary phase months earlier. There were no cost overruns and no blown budgets. Partnering can work in the building industry today if architects and contractors team together to give the owner the ultimate in construction cost accountability.

Counting the construction cost early is critical. Counting the construction cost accurately is critical. Counting the cost is not only an important element of the final financial considerations of the building program, but it is also a spiritual directive. "Who would build a tower without first counting the cost?" the Lord asks. He might as well said, "Who would build a church to further my kingdom to change their community without first analyzing the process and counting the cost?"

It is time that church architectural planners rise to the occasion, step up to the plate and be accountable to counting the cost early.

PROJECT BUDGETING

A good percentage of my time is often spent consulting with churches (who have used other architects) whose complete project costs have well-exceeded their original budgets. In most cases, these churches have concluded the preliminary design phase, master planning phase and the construction document phase with another architect often expending thousands of dollars. The plans have been bid out and only then are they aware that the costs of their project far exceed their architect's original estimate.

In other cases, churches will contact us with a similar story. They have completed their first phase of construction several years ago only to find that the ultimate cost of their project far exceeded their wildest expectations. The church spent thousands of dollars over and above their available financing. The debt service began to drive the ministry. In many cases, leadership lost credibility and in the worst of cases, churches split. Over our 25 years of experience, I believe that we have been able to identify the main culprit for most of these costing nightmares:

It is the difference between project budgeting and construction cost.

In many cases, a church building committee will begin to inquire from contractors or architects the probable construction costs for their construction project. But do they count the complete cost? Usually not.

There are many cost variables that are associated with the ultimate expenses of a construction project. The actual construction cost of the building itself, in reality, is only a portion of the total budget. In fact, we often utilize the following formula to communicate this concept to the local church:

> Construction Cost = 70% (to 80%) x Total Project Costs

Another way to state this formula is as follows:

> Project Costs = Construction Costs + 25%

If a church begins their master planning building campaign by analyzing the construction cost of the building only, they will already find themselves 25% over budget. So what are these additional cost factors which make up the substantial difference between the construction cost of the building and the total project costs?

Let's identify these additional costs briefly below:

1 > Architectural and other fees
There will be associated fees for professional services in order to provide the construction documents for your contractor. These may include the fees of the architect, structural engineer, plumbing engineer, mechanical engineer, electrical engineer, civil (site) engineer, landscape architect, acoustical consultant, as well as additional costs associated with projects such as soil borings, topographical surveys and boundary surveys.

2 > Landscaping
The landscaping includes the planting of trees, bushes and landscaped areas around the building and parking lots. In many cases, the minimum landscaping requirements are actually set by the comprehensive zoning ordinance of the municipality. The final landscaping is a cost of the project but often not included of the construction cost analysis of the building.

3 > Fixtures, furniture and equipment
In a project estimate, this is often referred to as F, F&E. In a typical church these costs might include pews or chairs, chancel furniture, choir chairs, tables and chairs for the Christian education wing, furniture for the administration wing, as well as the sound system.

4 > Contingency
In spite of proper planning and complete architectural services, there

will often be surprises through the building construction phase. Perhaps the contractor will find poor soil that was not identified on the soil tests under the proposed footings. Or perhaps the church building committee decides to change the layout of a few rooms. In the event of renovation, the contractor can often run into unforeseen situations. Due to this, it is often important to plan for a contingency fund.

5 > Construction loan costs

If the church is borrowing funds from a bank or mortgage company for the construction of the project, the actual loan is broken up into two different components. The 'construction loan' is the loan which the church borrows from the bank in order to make the monthly payments for construction to the contractor. The church will pay the bank interest on the loan amount based on their monthly draws. The construction loan cost is paid off at the end of construction with your permanent financing.

6 > Permanent financing closing costs

Once the project has been completed, the church will close on the permanent financing on the project, unless the construction cost was paid for in cash. Certain closing costs are always associated with permanent financing and will include points, closing costs from your lending institution, as well as legal fees.

As one can readily see from the above additional cost factors, there are many elements that comprise the actual project budget on a particular construction project. The following is a chart that we often utilize to further communicate the difference between project budget and construction cost:

ASSOCIATED COSTS

Construction Cost	Varies according to project
Architectural, Engineering and Associated Fee	8% – 12%
Landscaping	5% – 10%
Fixtures, Furniture, and Equipment	8% – 15%

NOTE: The above costs are approximate percentages for the typical church. It is not unusual for these costs to vary substantially depending on your church's particular project.

It is anticipated that the actual site development costs are already included into the construction cost above and therefore have not been listed as an additional associated cost. The site costs will often be 15% - 30% of the total construction costs and need to be identified early in the process.

As illustrated above, it is critically important to have your church architect evaluate your entire project budget. In the event that your building committee or leadership of your church has determined that you have $1 million to fund your project, remember that your $1 million cannot be the construction budget for the building. If the total finances available are $1 million, then you must count the costs of architectural fees, engineering fees, fixture, furniture, equipment, landscaping, contingency cost, construction loan cost and permanent financing cost. Once these associated costs have been identified, their costs will need to be subtracted from your overall budget to determine the final construction cost of the building itself.

FINANCIAL CAPABILITY

In an earlier chapter we discussed the Lord's parable concerning "counting the costs." I have already established the importance of counting the cost early in order to properly prepare for the building of the church project. However, it is important that the church not only "count the cost" of the construction project and associated cost, but it is also important that the church evaluate both the actual financial potential and capability of their congregation.

It is our experience that few churches have the financial resources that are needed to fully accomplish all of their ministry goals. If a church is growing and ministries are expanding, it is not uncommon for their wish-list and ministry needs to far surpass that of their actual available funds. In these cases, it is important for churches to prioritize their ministry needs in order of most important to least important. Phasing of the entire project can often help.

A determination of the financial capability of the local congregation is the starting point for the funding of a project. It is important for each church to carefully analyze the financial resources that are available to them for the actual building of the church. Pursuing the architectural process without evaluating the financial capability is a real mistake. One of the keys to a successful expansion program is to evaluate the project cost and financial capabilities simultaneously and match the two. No church wants to get caught in an expansion project with the total project budget seriously exceeding their financial capabilities.

In the process of determining the financial capability of an individual congregation, the following resources must be seriously evaluated:

1 > Available Cash
Many churches will begin to identify their particular growth in various areas of ministry well prior to any construction project. It is not uncommon for a local church, once they have identified ministry growth and facility needs to begin to allocate a certain percentage of their weekly budget to a building fund. Additional cash may become available through occasional surpluses of budget or special offerings. Cash available in a money market or CD will often lessen the financial strain and pressures of a building campaign once started.

2 > Weekly Budget Allocations
In a growing church, the actual income from weekly offerings may indeed create a surplus that could become available for project financing. Many of our clients have experienced tremendous ministry growth and have expanded their worship service from one meeting up to two or three meetings per Sunday morning. In many of these cases, the actual overhead and operating of the expenses of the church has remained fairly much the same, excluding another pastor or two on staff.

In this type of situation, the leadership of the local church can analyze the percentage of the church's budget that could be allocated directly towards facility planning. A general rule of thumb regarding the commitment of a percentage of your budget to debt retirement is often estimated to be 25% - 35% of your undesignated income. Obviously, the final percentage utilized by a local church can depend on a number of other factors.

3 > Capital Campaign Programs

Many of our churches have utilized capital fund-raising programs as a tremendous financial resource for their project. There are many different rules of thumb that are utilized for determining what the potential is of any particular congregation regarding capital fund-raising. The following has been communicated to us by fund-raising and capital campaign companies over the last many years:

The typical church can raise approximately 1.5 - 1.7 times its annual income over a 36-month period.

Many capital fund-raising companies throughout America and many denominations have their own campaigns for the local churches.

4 > Borrowing Potential

Very seldom is the local church in a position to pay cash for a particular project, though we have experienced clients from time-to-time that have built on a cash basis. In most cases, the local church will utilize their cash, budget allocations and capital fund-raising programs, as well as loans from a commercial bank or mortgage company for the remaining portion of the construction budget.

Obviously, there are many different opinions regarding the long-term indebtedness that a church can afford to incur. This is a spiritual issue and only the leadership of the local church can answer. It is important that the church, working hand-in-hand with their commercial bank officer or mortgage broker, determine the safe borrowing potential of their local congregation. As we stated above, one basic rule of thumb is that the church should never commit more than 25% - 30% of its undesignated income to actual loan payments.

In other cases, mortgage bankers will loan no more than 70% - 75% of the appraised values of the buildings and lands the church now holds. In other cases, we have known bankers to loan somewhere between 2.7 - 4 times the annual budget of a church. The borrowing potential of the local church and the entire question of whether or not a church borrows money for their program can be a sensitive issue and can only be determined through prayer and fasting of the local church leadership. The following are some preliminary budget formulas that can be utilized in order to give a church a preliminary estimate of their financial capability.

THE BORROWING POTENTIAL OF THE LOCAL CHURCH AND THE ENTIRE QUESTION OF WHETHER OR NOT A CHURCH BORROWS MONEY FOR THEIR PROGRAM CAN BE A SENSITIVE ISSUE AND CAN ONLY BE DETERMINED THROUGH PRAYER AND FASTING OF THE LOCAL CHURCH LEADERSHIP.

> **Current operating budget x 3 = Conservative Debt Limit**
    Example: A church with an annual budget of $300,000 would have a financial capability of borrowing approximately $900,000.

> **Current operating budget x 4 = Total Maximum Safe Debt Limit**
    Example: A church with an annual budget of $300,000 would have a financial capability of borrowing approximately $1.2 million

> **Giving Units x $4,500 per giving unit = Conservative Debt Limit**
    Example: 100 Giving Units x $4,500 per giving unit = $450,000

> **Giving Units x $5,500 per giving unit = Maximum Safe Debt Limit**
    Example: 100 Giving Units x $5,500 per giving unit = $550,000

> **40% Loan to Current Budget Ratio, then extended out 15 years at 8%.**
    Example: 40% x $300,000 yearly budget = $120,000 a year / 12 months = $10,000 per month payment as a maximum payment. (This $10,000 per month payment would be extended 15 years at 8%.)

> **70% Loan to Current and Proposed New Property Values Ratio.**
    Example: $1 million of current and proposed property values x 70% borrowing power = $700,000

Obviously, the above calculations are preliminary only and can best be determined by applying your own prayerful wisdom to your particular situation. We have had many churches identify their financial capability by evaluating their worship attendance times the increased weekly giving which is available from their congregation. Statistics can show that church's giving can be increased in the range of $5 - $7 per person per week. These figures are based upon worship attendance of men, women, and children.

Careful consideration should always be taken in establishing the financial capability of any church due to the fact that the ultimate financial capability figure will determine the construction cost of the project and ultimately the debt service of a that church for the next 10 - 15 years.

CHURCH FINANCING

Perhaps an entire book could be written on the concept of church financing and negotiations with the appropriate mortgage banking institutions. However, that is not the purpose of this section. I would like to identify some of the current approaches to church financing and address some critical issues at best. As you may have discovered by this point, many banks will just not loan money to churches for building campaigns. The major reason for this is the potential default on the part of the church. Banks don't like negative publicity and do not want to be in a position of having to foreclose on a church building.

In spite of the typical difficulty in acquiring church financing, there are many sources of financing that are readily available now to the local church. Most all of these could be explored depending on your need. The following are sources of church permanent financing available in today's financial arena:

> Commercial Banks
> Savings and Loan Corporations
> Some Insurance Companies
> Denominational Pension Funds
> Private Church Bonds
> Private Investors

> Mortgage Brokers and Bankers
> Non-Profit Foundation

A large percentage of our church clients ultimately borrow a percentage of the construction cost from a commercial bank. Bank loans are often for shorter periods of time and are often offered at a lower interest rate. However, we also have church clients that work through private mortgage bankers and savings and loan companies. Most commercial mortgage loans are amortized over 20 - 25 years in order to keep the cost to a minimum. However, the church can negotiate a lower interest percentage by agreeing to a balloon payment which requires them to pay off the original loan or refinance it at the end of 5 - 7 years.

Some of our church clients will actually work with their own denominations by acquiring denominational loans. Many of these are pension funds of the pastors that are paid to the denomination and then invested in the local churches. However, it should be noted that there are many more churches looking for loans than available finances in most situations.

Some of our churches have had success by offering bond financing within their own church. In this situation, investors that may be members or friends of the church can loan money directly to the church for a specific project funding and for a specified period of time. Many times there is a cost savings on bond financing due to the fact that the funds do not flow through any type of commercial banking institute. The individual bondholders for the church receive interest while the bond is outstanding and ultimately they receive back their entire principal cash amount when it matures.

Bond issues can provide churches with long-term financing at specific interest rates by utilizing available cash within their own congregation. It is important for the local church to note that church bonds are indeed a certificate of indebtedness and are often secured by first mortgage on the land and buildings, in addition to a pledge from the church to set aside a specific percentage of their budget on a monthly basis to actually retire this debt. Bonds can be issued in numerous denominations and are organized and offered through bondholders and licensed security dealers. When a local church has finally decided to seek a specific loan, different sources should be considered prior to selecting the one that best fits your particular needs. In any case, it will be important that the church put together a professional loan application.

The following items are often needed to grant a church loan from a lending institute and should be included within a bound loan application:

> IRS Tax Exempt Status
> Articles of Incorporation, Constitution and Bylaws
> Brief written history of the church
> Appraisals of existing buildings and proposed new land purchases
> Purchase contract, if appropriate
> Church loan application from the specific lending institute
> Audited income and expense statements for the past 3 - 4 years
> Balance sheets for the past 3 - 4 years
> Year-to-date income and expense statements
> Year-to-date balance sheet
> Income and expense projections, 5 - 7 years
> Attendance records, 3 - 5 years
> Resume of key church pastors
> Legal description of your property
> Copy of deed

Additional information that could be included within the application:

> Members list (Giving Units)
> Name and address of church accountant
> Leadership or administrative board, include deacons and elders
> Creditor list with name and address
> Banks with name and address
> Insurance policy statements
> Copy of note and mortgage
> Vicinity map showing location of church
> Photos of property or building
> Environmental study reports, if appropriate

In the event that the church project is new construction, the following items could be provided:

> Architect's name, address and telephone number
> Builder's name, address and telephone number
> Copy of construction contract
> Copy of architectural prints with all engineering documentation
> Book specifications from architect
> Detailed and itemized construction cost breakdown from the contractor

NOTE: The above list is a brief inventory of those items that have been required by lending institutes of our past clients. However, additional information could be required.

Obviously, much prayer, thought, fasting and consideration should always play a key role in the final selection of your lending institute. In many cases, your architect or contractor may have relationships with mortgage bankers and commercial loaning institutions, which they can recommend.

FUND-RAISING

We have been involved in a multitude of capital fund programs. In some of our churches, the local pastor and leadership of the church have led some programs. In other churches, experienced hired professionals have led other campaigns. In both cases, we have experienced that a capital fund-raising program can be a tremendous asset to the actual building and construction program of the church.

As we have already stressed, the fund-raising component of the building campaign can in actuality be a very significant spiritual event in the life of the local church. It often will promote unity amongst the church and can strengthen the individual membership.

It is not my objective here to completely cover capital campaigns and fund-raising procedures. However, we will touch briefly on several concepts that I believe are important to the success of your program.

Most capital campaign fund-raising programs are based on spiritual standards and are built on the following principles:

FUND-RAISING OFTEN WILL PROMOTE UNITY AMONGST THE CHURCH AND CAN STRENGTHEN THE INDIVIDUAL MEMBERSHIP.

> Stewardship is an important concept to be grasped by all the members.

> The principle of "equal sacrifices, not equal giving" is important.

> Each member of the church is to make financial commitments as a pledge.

> Adequately communicate the vision of the building program and proclaim how that fits into the overall vision of the church.

> Establish a well-developed and communicated program.

> Prior commitment principle (this principle is based on people making commitments before appealing to others to respond, such as leadership setting the example).

> Capital fund-raising campaigns often extend over a period of 2 - 4 months. There is the preparation and training of leadership mixed with the communication of the program's vision and the ultimate commitment. The fund-raising program often climaxes with the pledges being promised at a particular pledge-type service.

As we communicated in other portions of this chapter, most capital campaign fund-raising programs can raise approximately 1.5 - 1.7 times the annual income of the church over a period of approximately 3 years. We have experienced some churches that have raised less and other churches that have raised more.

Always remember that a capital campaign fund-raising program is much more than just raising funds. The act of exercising our faith, the act of moving into sacrificial giving and the act of walking in stewardship is real genuine worship. The wise men truly worshipped Him as they laid their gifts at the Lord Baby Jesus' feet. The widow in the temple truly worshipped as she gave her all, though it was only one mite.

Throughout your financial fund-driving efforts, never forget that the real effort is not just to raise funds for the construction of the project, but also to encourage your members to grow deep in God's Word regarding their resources.

Most capital campaigns will kick off the initial program with a three-month all-church program. However, the actual pledge period for the giving is recommended to be 2 1/2 - 3 years. Most of our clients have encouraged pledges to be paid on a weekly or monthly basis over and above the regular tithes and offerings.

The typical rate of return often varies from church to church. However, we have had several clients that have experienced an 80% - 90% return of their pledges. Some of our clients contact the people individually regarding their pledges and provide personal follow-up. Other churches frequently announce the percentage of pledges that have been received on a monthly basis.

In any event, it is my opinion that you should never start capital campaigns without the appropriate promotional materials included in your "vision casting" presentation. This is where the artistic 3-D computer modeled renderings of a professional church architect can play a tremendous role in the actual fund-raising of your project. It is not uncommon for us to present our 3-D renderings and, in some cases, present a computerized walk-through of their facility with the aid of our computer laptop and projector and hear the following responses:

IT WAS AS IF I COULD REACH OUT AND TOUCH THE VERY PEWS.

I COULD REALLY SEE US WORSHIPPING IN THAT SPACE.

IT WAS AS IF I WAS REALLY THERE.

If the master planning and architectural drawings accurately reflect your ministry needs, your church membership will embrace the plan. If the 3-D virtual reality computer models adequately convey the reality of the proposed physical structure, it is easier for the church membership to grasp a hold of the vision of the church's leadership.

Appropriate architectural renderings, necessary artistic drawings and visual aids illustrating fund-raising goals and, in some cases, actual models mixed with "prayer of the saints" will result in a successful campaign. It is my opinion that any attempt of "vision casting" without these helps from your church architect will be futile.

SUMMARY

The church has two major roles to play once they select their architect and begin their design process for a new church:

1 > The church must assist the architect in identifying and analyzing their ministry needs and the vision that God has given them for their particular church.
2 > The church must work with the architect to ultimately consider the financial capability of the church to handle such a building program.

The ultimate construction cost of the master plan must be equal to the availability of funds from that particular congregation. Otherwise, the catastrophe of a future debt service driving the ministry of the church can ultimately occur.

It is important to realize that the Word of God establishes Biblical principles regarding stewardship and costing accountability. It is also important to understand that "counting the cost" is not only a Biblical directive, but a critical aspect of the master planning process.

It is consequential for the church to determine the best process to be utilized for counting the cost prior to planning or building.

THE ACT OF EXERCISING OUR FAITH, THE ACT OF MOVING INTO SACRIFICIAL GIVING, AND THE ACT OF WALKING IN STEWARDSHIP IS REAL GENUINE WORSHIP.

> Do they wish to base the success of their building campaign on a square foot analysis of a local non-church architect?

> Are they willing to accept a loose preliminary estimate from a contractor that's not familiar with their needs?

> Or, is it best to hire a church professional that can analyze your ministry needs, assist you with your financial capabilities and, ultimately, put a program together that will meet the objectives of both?

It is important to understand the difference between construction costs and project costs. A professional church planner and architect can assist the local church with the evaluation of architectural fees, engineering fees, testing, civil engineering and boundary surveys, fixture furnishings and equipment, landscaping, construction and permanent financing closing costs. A church can only properly "count the costs" by evaluating all of the appropriate cost factors in a complete building program.

It is important that the church establishes their financial capabilities and then contact the appropriate commercial mortgage corporation for the construction loan in the event that such a loan is required. It is also critical for the church to evaluate the entire financial program of the master planning process in order to determine if a capital campaign fund-raising program is required.

The selection of the appropriate professional church-architect mixed with a prayerful consideration of the church's leadership can result in a successful building program that adequately matches the availability of funds with the project cost of the new structure. ■

SITE SELECTION 12
Planning Concepts and Design Considerations

PLANNING CONCEPTS AND DESIGN CONSIDERATIONS

For a new church or for a church that is relocating from its current location, one of the most important decisions that the church will face is the location of the new site within the city. There are many factors that should be taken into consideration when one begins the site selection process.

It is my experience that many churches purchase a site through a local realtor, close on the piece of property and then contact an architect to build on the site. By the time the local church planner or church architect is involved, the following concepts have seldom been addressed:

> Visibility
> Frontage
> Curb appeal
> Soil considerations
> Appropriate acreage needed for present and future growth
> Expansion potential

I believe it is very important that a church looking to purchase property first contact a church architect and design specialist to assist them in the site selection process.

The following are critical design factors that must be taken into consideration prior to purchasing property for a church:

ACCESSIBILITY TO HIGHWAYS

Research has shown that many people will only drive 10 - 15 minutes to attend what they feel is a "local" church. Though this is the norm, obviously there are situations whereby individuals may drive 30 minutes to an hour to arrive at a particular congregation of their choice.

Nevertheless, 60% - 80% of your congregation will want to drive no more than 10 - 15 minutes to arrive at your church. It is important to look at the current highway status and the availability of roads from the highways that lead to your particular site. In the event that the site is difficult or tricky to get to, many first-time visitors may get lost and ultimately give up on finding your church.

I BELIEVE IT IS VERY IMPORTANT THAT A CHURCH LOOKING TO PURCHASE PROPERTY FIRST CONTACT A CHURCH ARCHITECT AND DESIGN SPECIALIST TO ASSIST THEM IN THE SITE SELECTION PROCESS.

ADJACENT NEIGHBORS

We recently had a church that decided to locate on a beautiful piece of property on a perfect street. The traffic flow was great and the visibility was strong. However, the site was directly adjacent to an adult bookstore. Offensive neighbors will deter new members from attending your church. It is important that your church architect study the existing site that you are considering, as well as studying all neighboring properties in order to best consult with you regarding the purchase.

AIR-BORNE NOISE POLLUTION

Close location to the flights of airplanes, as well as major highways, can create incredible noise levels creating difficulties for a worship experience on some sites. Noise problems can not only be a deterrent to worship, but also can extremely devalue the property value over time.

AMOUNT OF ACREAGE

It is very important to study the mission of the church, the vision that God has placed upon your pastor, as well as your ministry needs current and projected over the next 5, 10, 15 and 20 years. Only by a planning study of this sort will one be able to ascertain the amount of acreage that is suitable for your present facility, as well as your long-range plans.

CONTINGENCIES TO THE CONTRACT

It is important to insert contingencies into purchase contracts in order to protect the potential buyer from eventual site problems. The following is a brief listing of contingencies we have used from time to time.

CONDITIONS

Buyer's obligation to perform this agreement is expressly conditioned upon the following:

> A complete development "Feasibility Study" will be obtained by the BUYER at its sole expense to assure the BUYER of the availability of public utilities, market sales data, drainage, engineering constraints, wetlands and other environmental considerations, etc. Same must be completely acceptable to the BUYER at its sole discretion or the BUYER may declare this contract null and void with a full refund of the earnest money deposit.

> BUYER being able to obtain all governmental zoning and approvals necessary for the construction and development of the Property. All required approvals shall be pursued at the sole expense of the BUYER. SELLER further agrees to sign all necessary preliminary plats and any necessary paperwork needed or required by the City of _____, State of _____, or any other governmental agency.

> SELLER hereby grants unto BUYER the right to go on the Property for the purpose of engineering, soil boring, inspections, erecting a sign to advertise the sale of developed lots, perform any and all

activity permitted under an Erosion and Sediment Control permit prior to the date of settlement. BUYER is granted the right, freely and at all times, prior to settlement, to go upon or to send upon the property surveyors, engineers, architects, contractors, planners or other agents, for the purpose of giving estimates, making surveys, inspections, soil test and boring, taking measurements and photographs, etc.

> BUYER agrees to use all diligence in applying for and obtaining bank financing to provide acquisition and development funding. If bank financing cannot be obtained on conditions acceptable to BUYER, at its sole discretion, then this contract shall be null and void and the earnest money deposit shall be refunded to BUYER.

> That the Buyer is able to obtain all governmental zoning, conditional use permit, site plan, or other approvals necessary for construction and development of the Property as intended by the buyer. All required approvals shall be pursued at the sole expense of the Buyer. At the date of settlement, all taxes and interest are to be prorated as of the date of settlement. Settlement is to be within thirty (30) days of both the Conditional Use Permit and the site plan approval by the City of _____.

> Review of the actual boundary line survey on the property and the Buyer's approval of all exceptions to the title contained in the title report.

> The Property has tested negative for hazardous wastes, toxic materials or any other substance, which would be damaging to the environment or which would have to be removed prior to or in the course of development.

> That the Property does not require a wetlands permit, and that a letter to that effect is received from the Corps of Engineers.

DESIGNER'S AND ENGINEER'S CLARIFICATION NOTES REGARDING CONTINGENCIES & PRELIMINARY DESIGN

Feasibility Study

The design firm will determine more precisely the specific requirements of the City of _____ for the development of this property. The primary goal of this TASK is to determine whether or not there are unforeseen criteria which would cause the site unable to be built upon.

a > We will investigate City improvement requirements for storm drainage, sanitary sewer, water, and right-of-way. We will address the pertinent issues with each department at the City and determine whether or not any issues related to their specific area of concern would render the site undevelopable.

b > Our experience has been that we will not be able to affirm the City's responses via a letter from them or confirming signature on our correspondence. Likewise, as City ordinances and policies can, and do, change frequently, the only certain definitive indicator of improvements necessary will be final, approved construction plans.

c > If analysis of off-site systems such as storm drainage outfalls, sewer pumping stations, or the like are necessary, our report will only address the likelihood of whether or not the problems are insurmountable or possibly economically unfeasible. The final studies, if required, will be accomplished with the site plan design TASK, which will only take place if the feasibility study yields favorable results and the Conditional Use Permit is obtained for the property. Should it become necessary to complete one of the aforementioned off-site system studies before making a final decision on going forward, additional design fees will have to be negotiated to our proceeding.

d > You may desire, and it may be stated in your sales contract, that other studies are necessary which are beyond the scope of the services we provide. We can procure separate consultants to furnish separate studies on these items. Wetlands, hazardous waste and environmental impact are common elements, which are usually resolved prior to closing on any parcel of land. An environmental consultant would perform these studies.

e > You may also be concerned with soil conditions on the site as relates to building foundation conditions, and permeability and water table conditions for implementation of a Beat Management Practice on-site. They would require a soils consultant which we could also coordinate for you and procure a proposal for the necessary services. They would provide soil borings to cover any possible location on-site for the building. A geotechnical report would be provided based upon the results of those tests elucidating their findings with recommendation for the final structural design or the building. They would also provide boring tests for proposed Best Management Practices facilities, which will be necessary to develop the site.

f > We will provide a written report for this TASK. We will present this report to the appropriate members of the church building committee when it is complete and provide five (5) copies for their use.

g > During the feasibility study, we can also assist you in preliminary design tasks in order to size the building and make certain that the site is adequate for the present and future long range growth of your particular project. This includes providing you with a clear and concise documented goals and objectives of the project, a complete space analysis and square footage statement regarding the size of the project, as well as a opinion of construction cost.

h > Once the items are complete, we can then provide a preliminary design, which would include floor plan studies and elevation studies of the entire project in accordance with the goals and objectives and square foot analysis as figured above.

i > At that time it may be appropriate for us to provide you with renderings, which would be 3-D realistic computer generated perspective renderings of your project including people, trees, cars, etc. At this point, we have significant data to provide a more *detailed opinion of construction cost specifically to you to assess in your building programming and planning.*

NOTE: The TASKS as outlined above are provided by both your architect and your civil engineer. Failure to utilize such professionals for the above services can prove detrimental to a new project.

CURB APPEAL AND VISIBILITY

It is very important when one considers a particular site, to view the site as you would approach it from an oncoming car. Visitors to your church have an opportunity to formulate their first impression while they are actually approaching the property from their vehicle.

If your particular property is located far back into the woods, it will be difficult for the architect to design your new project with adequate curb appeal. Visibility is very important to the future value of your church's land and to the growth of your church.

DIMENSIONS OF THE SITE AND LAYOUT

It is important when considering a new site to study the actual boundary of the site. Square and rectangular sites are much more usable than strange, odd and irregular sites. Such irregular shaped sites many times limit the development and the building of a church upon that piece of property. The efficiency of building per acre decreases drastically if a site is triangular or if it is long and narrow. It is important to study the site dimensions with your architect.

ENVIRONMENTAL CONCERNS

Over the last several years, environmental concerns have become more and more important in the selection of a site for a local church. One can never be too careful in evaluating all environmental aspects of a site prior to the purchase. In fact, our recommendation is to always include a contingency in your purchase contract to guarantee the lack of environmental problems. Environmental issues can range from oil spills to buried gasoline tanks on a site. We have had sites where asbestos was found from a 30-year-old dump, as well as problems with wetland issues.

The vegetation on the property will often dictate whether or not wetlands are available on the site. It takes a professional to identify wetlands grasses. In many cases, a phase 1 environmental study is required by the lending institution prior to closing. In the event that your lending institution does not require such an environmental test, you should contact your church architect immediately for consultation.

EXPANSION POTENTIAL

It is important that the piece of property meet the ministry needs that you are presently facing. However, it is also important that the property meet the acreage need of your 5, 10 or 15-year master plan. It is important that the acreage be suitable for the location of the buildings, as well as parking and outside green area. The architect can assist you in a complete master plan that will be instrumental in determining whether or not a particular site has potential for future growth.

FLOODING, DRAINAGE AND STORM WATER

It is important to have a civil engineer investigate your site regarding its proximity to flood plains and flood areas. Is it possible for the site to shed storm water run-off into an adjacent ditch or drainage easement? Has the site flooded in the past, and is there any uphill development that would create flood issues in the future?

Is the water table suitable, and do drainage requirements meet minimum standards for good planning? A church would not want to buy a site only to find out later that sump pumps are required and necessary to get the water away from the building.

FRONTAGE

For proper church planning, as well as for proper curb appeal, frontage on a street is important. Frontage is defined in linear footage terms and

references the amount of street frontage that is directly adjacent to your property line. Adequate frontage off the local street is important to assist in ingress and egress to the site from local roads. In many municipalities, the actual quantity of signage is based on the frontage of any particular site.

LEGAL CONCERNS

In many cases, we believe it is important that the church actually contact their attorney to investigate the particular site rather than depending directly on their real estate agent only. It is very important to make certain that the title to the site is available and free of all liens and encumbrances.

LOCATION WITHIN THE CITY

It is very important when considering the actual location of a particular site to take into account the neighborhood that you are considering. Are there other religious groups or denominations found around that particular site? What is the demographic layout of that particular neighborhood?

Is the property in a rural area or within the city? In most cases, property along corridors that attract office and retail will cost significantly more dollars per acre than those pieces of property located outside the actual city.

SITE TOPOGRAPHY

A near flat site is the most efficient site to build on. However, you don't want a site that is completely flat, as it will be difficult for your architect and engineers to drain the water off of your property. A slight slope on the property works best, which allows drainage to flow from the building to drainage, easements and ditches. Your architect and engineer can assist you in studying the topography of your land by pointing out any areas that could cause severe challenges for your building.

SITE UTILITIES-AVAILABILITY

Site utilities include sewer, natural gas, telephone, city water, cable and electrical service. Some properties in particular areas do not offer public utilities. In the event the sewer is not available on a particular site, the city will require significant site tests to be accomplished to determine if the soil is capable for handling a septic system. It is extremely important to study all potential sites in light of the utility connections and availability for that particular site.

SOIL CONDITIONS

All soils have inherent properties, which determine the soil bearing capacity of that particular soil once weighted with a building. Many soils are totally unsuitable for building upon. Your church architect can hire a testing company that will take soil samples of the site to answer the question of soil suitability.

All contracts should be contingent upon a soil boring testing prior to closing. In the event that the particular soils on your piece of property are not suitable for typical spread footings, extensive pilings could be required in order to place the building on the site. This can increase a construction cost by hundreds of thousands of dollars.

VALUE APPRAISAL

It is very important to determine the value of the site prior to purchase. The seller should provide you with a complete appraisal of the property.

If the property owner does not have a current appraisal, you have one or two options. You can contact the city in order to ascertain the tax value of the particular site.

You can also hire an appraiser to provide you with a professional appraisal of the piece of property. One way or another, it will be important for the church to protect themselves to make certain that your purchase offer does not exceed the value of the property.

ZONING ORDINANCES

Every city, county and municipality adopts a comprehensive zoning ordinance that often is written by the planning office, reviewed by the planning commission and passed and adopted by the local city government such as a city council. The zoning ordinance can set a number of requirements that can adversely affect property development of any individual site. The building setbacks of the rear property line, both sides and the front are always established by zoning ordinances.

The parking requirement, landscape requirement, as well as building to green-space ratio, are defined by zoning ordinances. We have had several churches that have purchased properties only to find out later that there were several zoning ordinances within their particular city that restricted the development of their church buildings on the site they purchased. Your church architectural planner can assist you in the review and study of all zoning requirements prior to purchase.

The local church should always use their realtor for the review of available properties in the geographical area of their interest. The realtor can be extremely valuable in finding properties that might be available for the church. We have found that an experienced realtor can not only advise the church of building sites that have already been listed by other realtors within the city, but also can find potential sites that may have not yet been offered up for sale. In the arena of site acquisition, the realtor is the professional and should be utilized by the church.

However, once certain sites have been identified for potential development, only the design professional with sufficient church experience has the training and the expertise to address the important site issues as discussed above. Proper site evaluation and final selection can be difficult, at best, and raises certain challenges that must be addressed by the professional.

A proper mix of the realtor's experience, proper planning by your church architect and appropriate prayer from your parishioners will always result in God's blessing and direction for your church's new site.

It is the first step towards your new facility, and God will direct you. Use proper planning and the wisdom that God has provided your design professional. God wants to bless you. God will bless you and you will occupy the land.■

SUMMARY 13

Where Do We Go From Here?

THE REAL CHURCH....

It is important to note again that the "real church" is not the buildings or the structures that we have discussed throughout this book. The church of Jesus Christ is not the sanctuary, fellowship hall or classrooms. God's Spirit does not dwell within the walls that we construct. God's Spirit dwells within our own spirit and we are the real sanctuary or dwelling place of the Lord. The Word of God is clear in the defining of the dwelling of God's Spirit. Consider the following scriptures:

"God doesn't live in temples made by human hands."
— Acts 17:24

"Don't you realize that all of you together are the house of God, and that the Spirit of God lives among you in his house?"
— I Corinthians 3:16

"Your body is the temple of the Holy Spirit."
— I Corinthians 6:19

"We who believe are carefully joined together with Christ as parts of a beautiful, constantly growing temple for God."
— Ephesians 2:21

It is clear from these scriptures that the church today is composed of us believers who worship God in spirit and truth. God dwells within our spirit, and His body is the church and we are His body. However, from early days, the church (meaning the true body of believers) would congregate together as encouraged by Paul's Epistles.

In fact, the early church, as reflected in Acts, met in the believers' households. They met regularly to break bread, read scriptures, encourage one another, praise and worship God and fellowship with one another. The temple was reserved for Jewish worship and the new Christians would meet and congregate outside of the actual temple grounds. During the early first century history of Christianity, the word "church" always referred to the body of believers. The word "church" was never used to refer to a building or the actual place of the assembly.

The word "church" actually comes from the Greek word, "ekklesia," which means "called out." Therefore, as we have already stated, the church is the "called out ones" or the born again believers. In today's society, the actual word "church" can hold various meanings as follows:

> It is used to signify the entire mystical body of Christ. The church was purchased with Christ's own blood (Ephesians 5:25-27).

> It can refer to a particular denomination such as the Southern Baptist Church, Episcopal Church or Catholic Church.

> It can also refer to the sum aggregate of the entire grouping of all denominations meaning all of those followers of Christ.

> Occasionally, the word "church" refers to a single independent group of Christians meeting regularly to worship God.

> We also use the term to refer to the actual buildings and the physical structures that are designed and built to house Christians during their group worship, corporate praise and other social activities.

Though this book has often utilized definition number 5 above, we quickly recognize that the buildings we design and build are only the structures used to encapsulate and enclose the activities of the real church, the body of Christian believers. We acknowledge that we, His people, are the real church. However, in today's culture and church climate, physical structures play an important role in the actual ministry of the local church.

THE ROLE THE BUILDING PLAYS

We have now firmly established, in scripture, that the church is the body of believers and not a physical building. However, most churches (body of believers) meet in actual physical locations and buildings. Though some new 'starter' churches meet in schools and others might meet in renovated shopping centers or even in the home of one of the believers, buildings are built daily to house the church.

The main purpose of today's church building is the sanctuary space which houses worship. In fact, I believe that one of the central purposes of the corporate church today is in the group worship, which takes place within built sanctuaries. Within the architecture of the entire building complex, the actual worship space should be paramount. This often happens through the design of the church steeple, the design of the large volume of the sanctuary space or the bell tower or spire. The expression of worship within the architecture is often stated and signified through the design of the sanctuary space.

The buildings and architectural style of the local church today also express the identification and personality of the church. The type of architecture can clearly provide an element of identification. The personality, mission, vision and styles of worship can be expressly communicated through the design. The actual design of the building structures can, in fact, speak volumes regarding the identity of the church worshipping within the building.

The architectural design of many Southern Baptist Churches often utilize the following design features:

> Red brick
> Large colonial wood columns at the entry
> Elaborate interior and exterior wood trim
> Large high white steeple
> Visually, a very religious looking building
> Smaller chancel with privacy rail with a piano and organ

In comparison, the architectural design of many Independent Charismatic Churches utilize different design features as follows:

> Contemporary styling
> Openness in the plan
> Community building style
> Large open chancel design for pageantry, orchestras and plays
> Most of the time, there is no steeple
> Contemporary spires

Obviously, these are only examples of some of our architectural responses to church clients, as most all designs vary a great deal based on the needs of the individual group of Christians. Nevertheless, in most all cases, the church building does reach into the sky as if reaching to God Himself. Whether the church has a spire, a bell tower or a more traditional steeple, the design element most always reaches into the sky, points upward and establishes a strong 'spiritual' focal point within the community. It stands tall always reminding us of Him, who designed us for His glory.

YOUR FIRST STEPS

The first realization that a local church needs additional space is the awareness that a required ministry need is not being met. Perhaps the children's department has outgrown the physical facilities of the education building. Or perhaps, a new senior's ministry has been birthed within your church and there is no space to facilitate their required activities. Ministry needs should always be a prerequisite to the building

MINISTRY NEEDS SHOULD ALWAYS BE A PREREQUISITE TO THE BUILDING OF STRUCTURES.

of structures. In this way, buildings are an expression of ministry needs and become a declaration of what God is doing within a local church. It is important for the leadership of a local church to establish a mission statement and document the vision that God has for their particular congregation. In this way, the final buildings and structures can be an expression of ministry needs within the defined context of the church's clear goals and objectives.

Once a ministry need has been identified and the church has clearly defined their God-given mission, it is time to select an architect to guide you through the process. It is vitally important that your final selection of an architect considers the architect's direct church design experience. My architectural firm has provided services on over 280 church commissions. However, we are still growing in our experience and wisdom relating to effective and efficient sanctuary design. You will need a church architectural design specialist to guide you through the complicated maze of master planning, preliminary design, design development, city and municipal approvals, construction drawings and the building and actual construction of your new church. Your selection of a church design specialist is one of the most important and critical decisions facing you and your leadership team.

Once you have selected your church architect, you are ready to begin the first phase of preliminary design. The architect will assist the church in the formulation of goals and objectives and in the shaping of your construction budget. It will be important to identify the phases of a project that are appropriate to your project. Your architect can assist you as well in this area. The preliminary guidelines, included in Chapter 10, can assist you in this area. The architect should ultimately assist you in the actual "vision casting" of your vision to your congregation. This is really a spiritual event in the life of the church.

WALKING IN UNITY

The unity of your church board and leadership is important in these beginning stages of your building project. It is equally important that you feel comfortable with your architect. This is a marriage-like relationship that will grow throughout the design phase and construction phase of the project. The length of the process may be as long as 2 years. Therefore, it is important that your leadership and your architect can work in unity with one another. Sharing of ideals, sharing of the Christian faith and a genuine love and concern from your design professional is consequential as you begin your project.

The Lord prayed for the unity of the church. His extraordinary intercession for Christian unity can be found in the following scriptures:

"

I WILL REMAIN IN THE WORLD NO LONGER, BUT THEY ARE STILL IN THE WORLD, AND I AM COMING TO YOU. HOLY FATHER, PROTECT THEM BY THE POWER OF YOUR NAME--THE NAME YOU GAVE ME--SO THAT THEY MAY BE ONE AS WE ARE ONE.
— JOHN 17:11

"

"My prayer is not for them alone. I pray also for those who will believe in me through their message, that all of them may be one, Father, just as you are in me and I am in you. May they also be in us so that the world may believe that you have sent me."
— John 17:20-21

"I have given them the glory that you gave me, that they may be one as we are one: I in them and you in me. May they be brought to complete unity to let the world know that you sent me and have loved them even as you have loved me."
— John 17:22-23

Christ prayed that the church might be one as He and His father are one. Unity is an important characteristic within the church in all situations. However, the design and building phase of a structure contains many challenges for the typical church leadership. It can be a formidable task for the best of leadership teams. Due to the possible difficulties that the growing church faces, it becomes critically important for the leadership team and the church architect to be in perfect unity.

This does not mean that we always agree on each decision. It does mean, however, that a spiritually unified team, bathed in prayer and intercession, makes each decision walking in love and acceptance for one another. Christ prayed for the church. We too should spend some portion of each planning meeting praying for this unity as well. The degree of unity in which the leadership team walks through the design process is often reflected in the church's response to the final design presentation. It is called modeled leadership.

Even Paul addressed the spiritual concept of unity in Ephesians. Consider the following scripture:

"As a prisoner for the Lord, then, I urge you to live a life worthy of the calling you have received. Be completely humble and gentle; be patient, bearing with one another in love. Make every effort to keep the unity of the Spirit through the bond of peace."
— Ephesians 4:1-3

Model the scriptural principle of unity within the leadership, and the people of the church will reflect this unity in both their response to the design and to the fund-raising of the project.

IT REALLY IS A SPIRITUAL EVENT

We addressed in Chapter 3 the spiritual aspects of the building process. It is easy for all of us to become focused on the physical aspects of the building delivery process. There are building committee meetings, planning commission meetings, city council meetings, design decisions to be made, color selections, pew selections, as well as a variety of decisions that are addressed throughout the entire building process.

It is easy to become lost within the physical 'building forest' that surrounds the journey. If one is not careful, challenges can be seen through physical eyes as merely a physical phenomenon. During difficult times, it is easy to view the city's planning staff or the city council as the enemy. The enemy of the church has never been the players in the building process. From the beginning of time, the church's enemy has been Satan. He was, is and will ever be the enemy of the cross.

During a difficult church building process, I will often stop, pray and ask God to enlarge and focus my spiritual vision and sensitivity. It is only then that I truly understand the spiritual perspective regarding a particular project. We must always be aware of our focus. In the midst of battle, it is easy to lose perspective. We must continue to ask God to shift our paradigm to that which He can see from the throne room.

Just as the Lord led Noah, Moses and Solomon, God will lead us as well.

Noah had no previous boat construction experience. But God gave him the plan.

Though Moses had construction experience from his earlier years in Egypt, he had never built a 'sanctuary' for God's presence. But God gave him the plan.

David had no architectural experience and Solomon had never built a temple before. But God gave David the plan and anointed Solomon for the occasion. The result was that God's Spirit filled the temple such that no one could enter.

The process is a spiritual journey. Yes, the final product is built from brick and mortar similar to Moses' building experience in Egypt. But the church building process is a spiritual one. We must always remember that this journey is always a spiritual one and that God will lead us through this pilgrimage.

ENJOYING THE EXPERIENCE

Though the design process can be a challenging one and the building process, at best, can be trying, God does lead us through the journey. As we focus on the spiritual aspects of the journey, "the peace that passeth all understanding," can fill our souls and make it an enjoyable experience.

God will bless and prosper the church as the church steps out to face the challenge. Consider the verse from Nehemiah:

> **"**
>
> I ANSWERED THEM BY SAYING, 'THE GOD OF HEAVEN WILL GIVE US SUCCESS. WE HIS SERVANTS WILL START REBUILDING...'
> — NEHEMIAH 2:20 A
>
> **"**

Always focus on the blessings of our God. It is He that will give you the success. We will arise and build because "the God of heaven will give us success..." It is an enjoyable experience. It should be an enjoyable experience. In fact, the whole process can be "joy unspeakable and full of glory."

Always remember the following:

> God will lead you in this building process
> God will direct you on your journey
> God can work through your Christian architect
> It is God's church
> Success comes from Him
> He has your vision in His mind's eye
> He will provide the finances
> Rest in Him and enjoy the process

As you walk through the process with a joyful heart, with an understanding that God has your vision in His mind's eye, you will enjoy the journey. As you reflect God's joy and peace, enjoying the walk with your Christian church architect and planner, others will perceive your enjoyment and will likewise model your walk as well.

The building process can be both an enjoyable and spiritual walk. Walk the walk, claim the scriptures and watch the salvation of our Lord.■

THE BUILDING PROCESS
CAN BE BOTH AN ENJOYABLE AND
SPIRITUAL WALK.

AN ARCHITECT'S PRAYER..."MY PRAYER FOR YOU!"

Lord,

You are the original architect and master planner of the universe. As You bless and grow Your Kingdom, Your church on earth will prosper and expand. As Your church expands, there will be need of physical spaces to envelop and contain Your ministry here on earth.

As this occurs, bless Your church and their leadership that they may walk according to Your Word and precepts, concerning building. Might they plan according to the vision You have in Your heart for them.

Assist the church leadership as they select the right church architect to assist them on this challenging journey. Fill the architect with a vision from You. Fill him with a love for the church that he is serving. Might he serve in true humility, love and unity as he forms the architecture that will ultimately provide the enclosure for the corporate worship of You, "The Great I Am."

Save the church from building great edifices that brings man glory alone. Save the church from cost over-runs and poor stewardship regarding the use of Your finances. Might all that the architect and church leadership accomplishes together bring You glory and assist You in the building of Your Kingdom here on earth 'as it is in Heaven.'

Might we always serve You, allowing the Holy Spirit to work through us to bless Your church.

Amen.

Appendix

Congregational Needs Survey

Project Development Budget Worksheet

Glossary of Terms

"SAMPLE"
Congregational Needs Survey

Church Name: _____

Church Address: _____

City, State Zip: _____

Over the last several months, our church's leadership has sensed a growing concern regarding our present facilities. The mission of the church has been strong and the ministry of the church has been growing.

It has been obvious for some time now that the facilities are inadequate in allowing us to effectively minister to our people. The present facilities are also not capable of handling the projected growth which we feel we will experience over the next few years. The church leadership has prayed that God would give them direction and wisdom in making long-term critical planning decisions.

We believe in the vision of the church and believe that we most likely need to renovate (or build) in order to effectively accomplish our mission. However, no physical expansion program can be successful unless the hearts of the individuals which make up the church support it.

As the leadership team of your church, we have a desire to better understand what you think regarding these matters. The following survey will assist us in evaluating the needs of our physical facility. This survey will not only address the several areas of need but will also be utilized to assist you in prioritizing those needs that have been brought to light by our leadership team. Please fill out the following chart regarding your perception of need:

"SAMPLE" CONGREGATIONAL NEEDS SURVEY

Area of Concern	No Change Needed	Improvement Needed	Problem Area	Not Applicable	Comments
1 > Site Planning					
Parking					
Walks					
Picnic					
Recreation					
2 > Worship					
Foyer Size					
Orchestra Area					
Choir Area					
Platform Area					
Sound System					
Temp. Control					
3 > Christian Ed.					
Classroom Area					
Classroom Size					
CE Office					
Audio/Visual					
Library					
Storage					
Day-School Facility					
Nursery Area					
4 > Support Spaces					
Storage Areas					
Restrooms					
Handicap Access					
Drive-thru Canopy					
5 > Family Life Center					
Fellowship Area					
Social Area					
Kitchen Size					

"SAMPLE" CONGREGATIONAL NEEDS SURVEY

Area of Concern	No Change Needed	Improvement Needed	Problem Area	Not Applicable	Comments
5 > FLC cont.					
Storage					
Bride's Room					
Treasurer's Rm.					
Board Room					
6 > Admin. Areas					
Office Areas					
Office Size					
Workroom					
Kitchenette					
Storage					

In the following spaces please list, in order of priority, those items that you checked above and identified as problem areas.

Priority #1: _____

Priority #2: _____

Priority #3: _____

Priority #4: _____

Priority #5: _____

Priority #6: _____

Priority #7: _____

In the event that the worship space needs expanding, please list the number of seats that you believe we should plan for over the next...

5 years: _____

_____

10 years: _____

_____

In an evaluation of current facilities, one will often evaluate current ministries to determine if there are ministries that could benefit the community that are currently not being provided due to a lack of facilities. What ministries does the church currently have in place that you believe should be provided for in new facilities?

_____

_____

_____

Of the priorities listed above in terms of physical facility expansion and/ or renovation, please list those areas in which you would be willing to spend portions of the resources which God has blessed you with:

_____

_____

_____

_____

Other considerations or comments:

_____

_____

_____

_____

_____

_____

_____

Name: _____ Date: _____

"SAMPLE"
Project Development Budget Worksheet

1 > Land Costs
Contract-Land Cost
(Acres=_____)
Other _____   _____

_____

2 > Professional Fees
Architectural   _____
Mechanical, Electrical & Plumbing Engineering   _____
Civil Engineer   _____
Structural Engineer   _____
Other _____   _____
Other _____   _____

TOTAL PLAN DEVELOPMENT COST

3 > Site Development Costs
Topographical Survey   _____
Sewer Tap Fee or Septic System   _____
Water Tap Fee or Well   _____
Soil Testing   _____
Site Work   _____
Parking and Sidewalks   _____
Street Improvements (required by city)   _____
Water and Drainage Retention   _____
Clearing and Grading   _____
Fire Line   _____
Sewer and Water Lines   _____
Landscaping   _____
Contingency (5-15% recommended)   _____

"SAMPLE" PROJECT DEVELOPMENT BUDGET WORKSHEET

Other _____   _____
Other _____   _____

TOTAL SITE DEVELOPMENT COST

4 > Building Costs
Construction Estimate   _____
Contingency (5-15% recommended)   _____
Other _____   _____
Other _____   _____

TOTAL BUILDING COSTS

5 > OTHER COSTS
Pews or chairs   _____
Chancel Furniture   _____
Specialty Furniture   _____
Chancel Design/Decor   _____
Sound System   _____
Audio/Visual   _____
Kitchen equipment   _____
Interior Plantings/Landscaping   _____
Other _____   _____
Other _____   _____

TOTAL OTHER COSTS

6 > Loan Costs
Origination Fees/Points/Bond Fees
Closing Cost
Land Payoff
Other Mortgage/Loan Payoffs
Other _____
Other _____

TOTAL LOAN COSTS

TOTAL: PROJECT DEVELOPMENT BUDGET COSTS

GLOSSARY OF TERMS

Allowance
An amount established in the contract documents for the inclusion in the contract sum to cover the cost of pre-described items not specified in detail in the contract documents. It contains provisions that cost variations between such amount and the final determined cost of the prescribed item will be reflected in change orders appropriately adjusting the final contract sum.

Appraisal
When a church client is renovating or adding on to an existing facility, it is often important to have an appraiser provide an appraisal on the property. This is where a professional reviews the property and/or the plans in order to ascertain an estimate and an opinion of value on a particular piece of land or real estate. It is important to have this value prior to establishing long-range plans. The appraisal is most always a written statement of the opinion of real estate value of the parcel of property and/or building and is tied down to a specific date.

Arbitration
The binding resolution of disputes by one or more neutral persons (usually called arbitrators) as a substitute for judicial proceedings. This may be invoked only by agreement of the parties to the dispute but such agreements must be arrived at before there is an actual dispute.

Architect
An architect is an individual that has typically undergone college training in most every area of building design as well as engineering. Most architects have a total of 5 - 7 years of college experience and 2 - 3 years of internship prior to being required to sit for an extensive state exam in their particular state. Architects are required to undergo testing (which is approximately 5 full days) prior to being licensed in a state to provide services as a professional architect.

Asbestos
Asbestos is a fine, flexible, non-combustible, inorganic fiber obtained

from natural hydro-magnesium silicate. It can withstand high temperatures without change and is a poor heat conductor. This was utilized in many materials in the past. There are many federal and state laws at this point regarding the removal of such asbestos materials in a renovation type project.

Balloon Payment

A balloon payment within financing is a lump sum payment required by the lender that must be made at a specific point in the loan amortization schedule. For example, a thirty-year amortization schedule could have a balloon payment of the remaining principle balance due at the end of 10, 15 or 20 years.

Bidding

Once the architect completes the construction documents, the owner will occasionally have the architect contact several contractors for competitive pricing. The architect will most typically allow the competitive bidders to utilize 3 - 4 weeks in obtaining quotes on all aspects of the work from their sub-contractors and material suppliers.

Bidding Requirements

Those documents provided by the architect, which provide information and establish procedures and conditions for the submission of all bids. They often consist of the notice to bidders and advertisements for bid, instruction to bidders, invitation to bid and typical sample forms.

Bid Opening

The opening and tabulation of bids submitted by the prescribed bid time and in conformity with the prescribed procedures as set forth by the architect.

Blueprint

A pre-production of a drawing by means of a contact printing process on light sensitive paper, producing a negative image consisting of white lines on a blue background. However, it often refers to reproductions of architectural drawings or working drawings which are utilized on the construction sites, which are actually blue lines on white paper. The process of reproduction is similar.

Bonding Company
A bonding company is a corporation licensed to handle the legal requirements of issuing bonds on the project.

Building Codes
Each state adopts a standard building code. There are several generic building codes that can be adopted by the various states including the BOCA National Building Code, the Uniform Building Code and the Southern Building Code. Most every state adopts a model national code that is modified for the local conditions. They may also have additional building codes and regulations which they will add to the National Building Code. It is very important that the church architect understands the building code which is adopted by your particular state. The building must conform to the state building code as well as to any additional city or county codes in order for a permit to be issued for construction.

Buyer's Market
This is a market in which there are more sellers than buyers in a particular financial climate. Prices tend to be low.

Cash Allowance
See "Allowance."

Cavity Wall
This is also referred to as a hollow masonry wall or a hollow wall. Most often in church construction, this is an exterior wall most always constructed of masonry consisting of an outer and inner withe separated by a continuous air space but connected together by wire or sheet metal ties. The dead air space provides improved thermal insulation, and in many cases, fixed insulation is also placed between this air space.

Chancel
This is the front portion of the church often including the pulpit, staging and choir area.

Chancel Arch

This is the traditional arch, which in many churches marks the separation of the chancel (or sanctuary) from the nave or the body of the church.

Chancel Rail

The railing or barrier in place of a chancel screen by which the chancel is separated from the nave.

Chandelier

This is a light or luminaire suspended from the ceiling which is usually of brass material, very ornate and branched with visible lamps.

Civil Engineer (Site engineer)

The civil engineer is a professionally trained individual that has most always gone to college for specialized training and then has been tested and licensed by his particular state. Their expertise includes entire site planning, drainage, utilities, exterior piping, as well as parking lots paving and curbing. The architect often coordinates this work by working specifically with a sub-consultant, who is a civil engineer on the project.

Commitment Fee

The commitment fee is a finance charge made by a particular lender in order to agree in the present to make a loan in the future. The lender is committed to making that loan when the loaned is required and such commitments are made up in writing and signed by all parties.

Construction Documents

Once the architect has completed the programming and master-planning phase of the project, he proceeds to the construction document phase. The construction document phase is the phase of the project whereby the architect adds all the details to the drawings, as well as dimensions and notes, to reflect his intentions of construction to the contractor. The drawings should be fairly complete and include the following:

> Floor plans
> Foundation plans
> Building elevations

> Schedules of doors, windows, and finishes
> Construction sections through the entire building
> Framing details
> Appropriate details

These drawings are then submitted for final client approval and then submitted to the city.

Construction Loan

Quite often the church will be in the position of borrowing money from a bank or mortgage company. The actual permanent financing is typically not fixed until after the construction project is completed. However, the owner will often need additional funds to pay the contractor through construction. Mortgage companies, to cover the expenses actually incurred throughout the building process, often provide this type of short-term financing. The financing is over a short-term period, which is usually 6 months to 1 year and is approved at a slightly higher rate than most permanent loan financing. The construction loan is then replaced by the permanent loan when the project is completed and the architect has approved the final building.

Construction Loan Draws

From time-to-time the contractor will provide a payment requisition to the architect for approval. Once the architect has approved this payment requisition, the owner will draw down against his pre-approved credit line from his construction loan for the payment of the contractor.

Construction Testing

Construction testing is utilized throughout the construction process to ensure the quality of the work of most of the sub-contractors. The tests are used to verify the compliance with the contract documents. There are many tests that the contractor can utilize including testing the strength of concrete used, the structural steel connections, weld, etc. The architect will almost always specify the type of tests that will be needed.

Contract Documents

see "Construction Documents."

Contractor

A contractor is an individual or company that contracts with the owner through the architect to build the actual project. He agrees to perform all or portions of the work as dictated on the construction documents in exchange for final payments from the owner.

Contractor's Liability Insurance

Insurance purchased and maintained by the contractor to protect him from specified claims which may arise out of, or result from, his operations under the contract. This is whether such operations be made by himself or by subcontractors or by anyone directly or indirectly employed by any of them or by anyone for whose acts any of them may be liable.

Contract Time

The period of time established in the contract documents and/or instructions to the contractor by the owner or architect within which the work must be completed.

Debt Service

The debt service is the sum of the interest and principle payments on a particular loan. This is often specified as a monthly or annual figure.

Dentils

One of a band of small, square, tooth-like blocks formed out of aluminum, wood, or stone forming part of the characteristic ornamentation of the ionic, Corinthian and composite orders. Often a dentil band, which is an uncarved band, will occupy the similar position in a cornice on a typical church of today.

Depreciation

This is an annual allowance for the use and the general wear-and-tear of a particular capital asset. This is a non-cash expense on your books.

Easements

It is always important to have the civil engineer inspect the entire property for the location of right-of-ways across that property. Many times these right-of-ways are permanent and are recorded at the local county or city planning offices. They have usually been purchased by the public or commercial entities. Quite often, these are utility companies that have utilities passing through the land that is to be purchased. They limit the use of the property and should be fully identified prior to the purchasing of any property.

Efflorescence

An encrustation of soluble salts, commonly white, deposited on the surface of stone, brick, plaster or mortar. This is usually caused by free alkalies leeched from the mortar or adjacent concrete or brick as moisture moves through it.

Elevations

The building elevations essentially are the views of the outside of the building. They are often utilized to communicate to the contractor the locations of door and windows, the heights of the walls, as well as the material selections for those walls. The appearance of the building is often seen in the elevations including height, rooflines, etc.

Entablature

In classical architecture, and often utilized in churches, this is the elaborate beam member carried by columns. This is horizontally divided into the architrave, which is the bottom portion of the entablature, the center which is referred to as the frieze, and the upper portion referred to as the cornice. The proportions and detailing are varied from order to order but are strictly prescribed.

Fire Protection

Materials, measures and practices for preventing fire or for minimizing the probable loss of fire by proper design and construction of buildings. The architect is trained in providing the adequate fire protection to meet the codes of any particular area.

Fire Protection Sprinkling System

An automatic system for protection against fire which sprays water over a large area in the event of fire. This consists of a piping system, which is often installed throughout the entire area, usually at the ceiling line to which sprinkler heads are connected.

Fire Resistance Rating

The time and hours that a material or a combination of materials in a particular construction can withstand fire exposure, as determined in conformity with generally accepted standards and derived from standard testings.

Fire Resistant Ratings

The rating of a particular material and the capacity of that material or construction (a variety of materials) to withstand fire or to give protection from it. According to OSHA, so resistant to fire that, for a specified time and under conditions of a standard heat intensity, it will not fail structurally.

Floor Plan

The floor plan is a view of the floor from above, showing the walls of the buildings and defining the locations of all the spaces. Most all of the drawings of the entire construction documents set are referenced from the actual floor plan. The doors, windows, finishes, wall types, room names and dimensions of the entire building, as well as individual spaces, are often shown there.

Furring

Strips of wood or metal, which is applied to rough surfaces such as concrete or concrete block so as to provide a flat plane which a surface material or assembly such as gypsum board or plaster, may be installed.

Glue Laminated Timber

A manufactured product often used in churches, consisting of 4 or more wood layers, none of which exceed two inches in thickness, bonded together with adhesive. This is often utilized in columns and beams exposed in church design.

Graduated Payment Mortgage

A graduated payment mortgage allows a church, which is expecting its growth, and therefore its income, to increase over time, to start out with much lower initial payments. The payments gradually get larger as the church grows. Quite often church bonding companies will offer this to the church clients. It is our experience that few banks are interested in such graduated payment mortgages.

Guarantee

A legally enforceable assurance of the quality or duration of a product or of the work performed. It is often also a binding commitment by one person or corporation that another will perform his contract obligation satisfactorily.

Guaranteed Maximum Cost

This is an amount established in a written agreement between owner and contractor as the maximum cost of performing a specified work on the basis of cost of labor and materials, plus an overhead expense and a profit fee.

Half-Column

This is an column projecting approximately one-half of its diameter, and sometimes usually slightly more, which is placed adjacent to a brick and/or masonry wall. This is often utilized in church design.

Interest-Only Period

This is a term used in which the interest only is charged on a particular loan by a lending institute. At the end of a pre-determined term, amortization may begin or the entire principle may be due. A construction loan, which the church borrows for the use of the construction period, is often an interest-only loan.

Interior Finishes

The exposed interior surfaces of building walls, such as plaster or wood. This often can refer to applied materials such as wallpaper, paint and trim. All interior finishes are classified according to ASTM tests for the surface burning characteristics of such materials. Class A being the best and Class E being the poorest in ability to resist fire spread.

Legal Interest Rate

Legal interest rate is the maximum interest rate that may be charged for a loan in a particular state. This law may also specify a maximum amount and the term allowed for such repayment of the said loan.

Loan Commitment

This is a written statement from the lender in response to a formally executed loan application in which the lender agrees to lend a specific amount of money for a specific rate of interest over a specific period of time. In most cases, this real estate loan commitment must state the amount of the loan, the term of the loan, the interest rates, the fees if any, the conditions and requirements for the funding and the real property to be taken as a security. All parties sign this commitment.

Loan Package

This is a collection of documents that the church puts together for the lending institute relative to a specific project and/or property. The lender will base their loan decision whether to approve or decline a loan request on this loan package. In some cases, this is referred to as a permanent loan portfolio.

Market Value

This is defined as the highest price, estimated in terms of dollars, which a property will bring if exposed for the sell in an open market. It is often viewed as the highest price that would be paid allowing for a reasonable time for finding a purchaser who would buy such real estate and/or property/buildings with full knowledge of all the uses to which it could be adapted and for which it is capable of being used in the present as well as the future.

Master Planning

The master planning process has been defined more specifically in a chapter within this book. However, it is during the master plan design process that the architect will guide the church through the entire process of designing for the present, as well as planning for the future. The master planning process should identify the goals and objectives, as well as all budgetary constraints for this phase and future phasing.

Mechanical, Electrical and Plumbing Engineering

The architect will most often coordinate the mechanical, electrical and plumbing components of the building with a sub-consultant that is an engineering specialist in this area. He will provide such drawings on the project to communicate the needs of all of these systems to the contractors. The mechanical sheets will explain the heating, ventilating and air conditioning of the entire project including duct sizes. The electrical sheets will often show the lighting, the power and the electrical panels, fixture types and locations throughout the building. The plumbing sheets will be utilized to identify and locate components of gas systems, sewage systems, water and other components.

Mechanical Engineer

A mechanical engineer is also a trained professional individual that has been tested and licensed by the state in which he practices. The mechanical engineer is specialized in mechanical systems, which include air delivery systems, cooling systems, electrical distribution systems, plumbing systems, drainage systems, pneumatics, conveyors and cooling systems.

Mechanic's Lien

A lien on privately owned real property created by states statute in favor of person supplying labor and materials for a building or structure or improvements thereon. Generally, it is placed for the value of the labor and materials supplied by them which has not yet been paid. In some states, mechanic's lien also exists for the value of professional services. Laws differ greatly among states as to the circumstances in which that the lien may arise. In most circumstances, a clear title to the property cannot be obtained until the claim in which the lien is based has been settled.

Millwork

These are ready-made products which are manufactured at a wood-mill or woodworking plant including doors, doorframes, window sashes, moldings, stair work, cabinets, etc. Normally this does not include flooring, ceilings and/or siding.

Mortgage

In short, mortgage is a debt security. Conveyance of property by a debtor (mortgager) to a creditor (mortgagee) as security for the debt, with provision that it shall be conveyed on payment of debt within a certain period of time, as agreed to in writing. The delivery of the deed will affect this. When the mortgage is completely paid off, the pledge is dead.

Mortgage Banker

Mortgage banker is a corporation, or in some cases an individual, having a relationship with one or more institutional bankers or lenders. The lenders generally expect a certain minimal annual volume of business from their correspondents and expect the correspondent to service all loans it places with the lender.

Mortgagee

The lender in a mortgage loan transaction.

Mortgager

The borrower in a mortgage loan transaction.

Narthex

An enclosed porch or vestibule at the entrance to the church. It is often referred to as a lobby or airlock entry.

Nave

The nave is the middle aisle of the church. Also, this is the center part of the church intended primarily for the laity and often includes the middle and side aisles of the church from the entrance of the church to the crossing or the chancel area.

Open Bidding

The submitting or receiving of bids from all interested contractors. This is seldom utilized on church projects.

Pediment

In classic architecture, as well as current church architecture, it is the triangular gable end of the roof above the horizontal corners. It can also refer to a surface used ornamentally over doors and windows and openings, usually triangular, but also can be curved.

Pedestal
A support for a column, statue, urn, etc. consisting often in classical architecture of a base, cornice and cap. Often, in modern design a plain block without ornamentation is utilized as a pedestal.

Prime Rate
The prime rate is defined as the interest rate charged by commercial banks to prime commercial loan customers. The interest rates for such church loans are often offered at prime plus points. For example, if the prime percentage rate is 10% and the lender's rate is prime plus two, then the commercial loan interest rate would be 12%.

Professional Liability Insurance
Insurance designed to insure an architect or engineer against claims for damages resulting alleged professional negligence. A church should never work with an architectural firm that does not carry an appropriate amount of professional liability insurance.

Program
The program is the tool the architect utilizes to establish all of the parameters required in the particular project. It is during the programming phase that the architect will come up with written documentation and lists of the goals and objectives, as well as all of the major spaces required throughout the entire facility.

Project Punch List (project closeout)
At the completion of the project, the architect will walk through the entire facility with the owner. He will look at the entire construction of the project, as well as the finishes on a room-by-room basis. The final punch list is a listing of all of the areas of construction that need to be fine tuned or completed prior to the architect stating that the project is substantially complete.

Resilient Channel

In sound insulating construction, which is often utilized around sanctuaries or Christian education spaces, a fabricated metal strip having two faces with flexible inter-connection can often be utilized for attaching gypsum board to studs and joists without a solid connection. This reduces the transmission of noise and vibration from one space to another. Often resilient clips are utilized for the same sound-insulating construction methodologies.

Rule of 72

The Rule of 72 is a method that is commonly used in computing the time at which money will double at a particular interest. This is often utilized in fund-raising events when one considers investment value of cash on hand. For example, the Rule of 72 states the following:

(You divide the interest rate into 72. For example, 6% interest into 72 = 12 years. The Rule of 72 would state that money doubles in 12 years invested at 6%.)

Scale

This is a system of proportion utilized by architects and engineers by which definite magnitudes represent the defined larger magnitudes. Most all drawings are scaled, usually considerably reduced in size from the actual design object or building. Quite often architects will utilize the scale of 1/8"= 1' or 1/4" = 1' for floor plans and elevations. Other scales, usually much larger, are utilized by the architect for larger scaled details.

Schematic Design

The schematic design is the phase of the project whereby the architect provides a preliminary layout of the entire building design and site design for the client to review. The purpose of this is to make certain that components of the building are in proper relationship to one another. It is also important to make certain at this phase that the architect satisfies the requirements of the program.

Seal

This is a stamp or embossing device utilized by design professionals, architects and engineers. These are almost always located directly on the drawings and specifications as evidence of his registration in the particular state where the work is being performed.

Sections

There will be a variety of sections utilized by the architect which are very similar to cut-throughs made through the entire building. This shows the contractor the interior construction of the various wall components, roof components, and how all the parts fit together. The details are used specifically to explain how the actual building is to be constructed and the intent of the architect.

Select List Bidding

This is a submitting or receiving of bids from a pre-approved and pre-selected list of contractors on a particular church project.

Seller's Market

This is a market in which there are more buyers than sellers, where prices tend to be high.

Site Plan

The site plan is the set of drawings produced by the civil engineer on the project under the direction of the architect. It includes the physical survey, the boundary survey, as well as a topographical survey information on one plan. It also locates the building on the site plan and shows all aspects of the building (both present and future), as well as sidewalks, storm drainage, exterior signage, landscaping, parking lots and utilities.

Sound Transmission

The passage of sound from one point to another.

Sound Transmission Class

This is often referred to as STC. It is a single number rating of the sound insulation value of a partition door or window. It is derived from a curve of its insulation values a function of frequency. The higher the number, the more effective the sound insulation is.

Specifications

The specifications are certainly part of the construction documents. They are actually written descriptions of all the materials and methodologies to be utilized on the project. In some cases the specifications can be quite complex and ultimately be a book that is 3" - 4" thick. On other occasions, they may be as simple as a few pages to give the contractor direction. The architect should determine the complexity or simplicity of the specifications and the owner, based on the project type.

Structural Engineer

A structural engineer is also a trained professional individual that has been tested and licensed by the state in which he practices. The structural engineer is often coordinated and hired by the architect and is a specialist in designing the actual structure to hold the building up from the footing to the roof framing above. They are experienced in footing design, foundation design and structural components sizing of most all buildings.

Structural Plans

Structural Plans are utilized by the architect to convey to the contractor information such as the foundation, footing sizes, footing and foundation details, beam sizes and details of floor framing and roof framing. The entire framing system is sized with connection and structural details on the sheets. This is often handled directly by the architect, though he may utilize the services of a consultant.

Subordination

This is an act, by a party in the transaction, of taking an inferior position with respects to the rights to obtain something of value in a particular transaction with another individual and/or company or corporation. For example, a lender who subordinates his position to that of a new lender will have the rights to the property only after the new lender's debt is fully satisfied by that particular church.

Sub-contractor

A sub-contractor is a company or an individual that contracts for a smaller portion of the work under the direction of the specific general contractor or construction manager. This includes, but is not limited to, plumbers, mechanical sub-contractors and electricians.

Substitution

A material and/or process offered in lieu of, and as being equivalent to, a specified material or process as required by the architect. Quite often, a contractor will offer a substitution to the owner through the architect for consideration. The architect then determines whether or not the substitution in effect is actually equivalent to that which he has specified.

Surveyor

A surveyor is a trained professional licensed in his state for providing land surveys. He also prepares the actual legal documents, which are utilized by the owner and the owner's consultants for recording the exact boundaries and physical characteristics of the actual real estate. He provides physical surveys, which are an exact duplication of the size location and bearing of each property line. He also provides a topographical survey, which is a record of all elevations in the lay of the land.

Value Engineering

Value engineering should be utilized on most all projects by the architect and the contractor in order to find better ways to accomplish the same result while saving money. The concept of value engineering is that it can reduce substantially construction cost on a project.

Wallfurring

see "Furring."

Waiver of Lien

This is an instrument by which a person or organization that has, or may have, a right of a future mechanic's lien against the property of another actually relinquishes such right in writing.

Zoning Ordinances

Each county or city adopts a complete set of zoning ordinances, which are often referred to as comprehensive zoning ordinances. These are a set of restrictions which govern the way in which a particular piece of property within the city or county can be utilized. Most always the municipality has adopted a master plan for development of their entire city. This is usually done through the planning department and then approved by the planning commission and city council. The churches are often allowed in most all types of zonings as a non-conforming use. There are many regulations that can limit the actual church project. Many cities and municipalities require the architect to take the plans to the planning commission and city council for a conditional use permit. This is a permit based on some conditions which allow a church to build within a particular zoning area. It is very important to have the civil engineer completely investigate the zoning ordinance prior to purchasing a piece of property for the building of the church.

Notes

Notes

Notes

Notes

Notes

Notes